CUDDLY TOYS AND DOLLS

CUDDLY TOYS AND DOLLS

JEAN GREENHOWE

Hamlyn

London · New York · Sydney · Toronto

Acknowledgments

The toy designs in this book were originally featured in WOMAN'S WEEKLY magazine and the author would like to express her thanks to the editor and all home department staff for their assistance and co-operation during the preparation of this book.

The author and publishers also wish to thank IPC Magazines Ltd, publishers of WOMAN'S WEEKLY, for their kind permission to reproduce their photographs.

First published in 1982 by
The Hamlyn Publishing Group Limited
London · New York · Sydney · Toronto
Astronaut House, Feltham, Middlesex, England

Filmset in England by Tameside Filmsetting Ltd., Ashton-under-Lyne, Lancashire in 10 on 11pt Apollo.

Printed in Spain

ISBN 0 600 30529 5

CONTENTS

Tips for Toymakers   11

Large Soft Toys   19

Sit-upon Toys   55

Small Soft Toys   63

Rag Dolls   71

Rosette Dolls   99

Novelty Toys   119

List of Suppliers   139

Index   140

TIPS FOR TOYMAKERS

This book contains instructions for making well over forty toys, including rag and stockinette dolls (to dress and undress), large and small fur fabric animals, mascots and novelty toys and a set of rod puppets.
Wherever possible the patterns are printed full size and can be traced directly off the pages. For larger toys, the patterns are printed on grids for easy scaling up to full size.
Many of the toys included have proved to be firm favourites with WOMAN'S WEEKLY readers over the years, so I am especially pleased to see them all gathered together in one volume.

Instructions

First and foremost, do read the instructions! They contain all the information you need to make a toy just like the one shown in the illustration.

Safety first

Do make sure that the toy you are making is suitable for the person for whom it is intended. Very young children should not be given toys containing any dangerous items such as buttons or beads, which could become detached and swallowed. Felt eyes and noses are much safer than glass or plastic – however securely these may be fixed.

Equipment required

Dressmaking equipment: You need all the ordinary items as used for dressmaking – sewing machine, sewing threads, sharp scissors (a large and a small pair), sewing needles, tape measure, etc.
Ruler: Marked with metric and imperial measurements.
Pins: Large glass or plastic-headed pins are the best kind to use when making soft toys, as they are much easier to see and handle than ordinary pins. To avoid the danger of any pins being left in the toy accidentally, use a limited number and count them at each stage of making.

A delightful selection of professional-looking toys can be made by following the instructions carefully and bearing in mind these useful tips

Tweezers: These can be very useful when handling small pieces of fabric or felt – for example when glueing facial features in place.
Compasses: A pair of inexpensive school compasses will be found invaluable for drawing out small circular patterns. Very large circles outside the span of your compasses can be drawn as described in the section headed *Copying the patterns*.

Adhesive

Use an all-purpose clear adhesive such as UHU. This adhesive dries very quickly and also remains flexible after it is dry.

Before cutting out facial features from felt, first spread the back of the felt with a little adhesive, then work it in with the fingers and leave to dry. When felt is treated in this way the cut out shapes will have smooth well-defined edges.

Unwanted smears of this adhesive can be removed by dabbing with a cloth dipped in a little acetone. Take care when using acetone as it is highly flammable.

Measurements

The sizes given throughout this book have been worked out individually both in metric and imperial, so that in many instances the conversions seem to be inconsistant and measurements do not always convert accurately from one to the other. This rounding off of measurements is to avoid having awkward sizes when a little extra either way will make no difference whatsoever to the appearance of the finished toy.

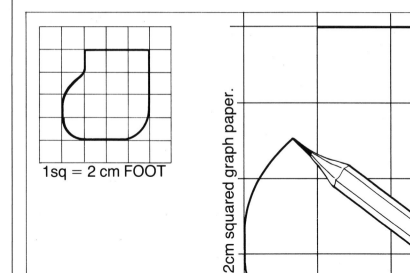

1sq = 2 cm FOOT

2cm squared graph paper.

Diagram 1 Drawing out full-size patterns on to graph paper from the scaled down diagram (shown above)

Copying the patterns

If full-size patterns are given for a toy, these can be traced directly off the pages onto thin strong paper, such as ordinary note paper. First follow any special notes in the instructions regarding the patterns, then after tracing and cutting out the patterns, mark on all details and lettering.

Patterns for the larger toys are given scaled down on grids ruled to represent 1 cm, 2 cm or 5 cm squares. For drawing out such patterns to full size, you can buy packets of dress-maker's metric graph paper from dress fabric shops. This paper is usually divided into 1 cm squares with a heavier line ruled at 5 cm intervals.

If the scaled-down diagram states 'one square = 2 cm', then use a coloured pen or pencil to over-rule the graph paper every 2 cm. Now, following the scaled down pattern outlines square by square, draw the same shapes onto the 2 cm graph paper as shown in diagram 1. Follow the same procedure for 1 cm and 5 cm squared diagrams.

For circular patterns the measurement given is usually the diameter (the distance across the centre), of the circle. When drawing circles set your compasses to the

radius measurement, i.e. *half* the diameter. To draw circles which are larger than your compasses can make, take a length of thin string and knot one end round the point of a pencil. Now tie a knot in the string, the required radius measurement away from the pencil point, keeping the string taut as you measure. Now draw the circle as shown in diagram 2.

When measurements for simple shapes (such as squares, rectangles or triangles) are given in the instructions, you can draw these directly onto the wrong side of the fabric

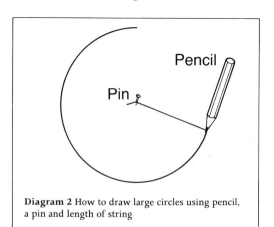

Pencil

Pin

Diagram 2 How to draw large circles using pencil, a pin and length of string before cutting out. However, if the toy is to be made more than once, it is a good idea to cut paper patterns for such shapes and mark on all the details for future use.

Seams

Seams and turnings are allowed on the pattern pieces as stated in the instructions for each toy. Join fabric pieces with right sides facing unless otherwise stated.

Fur fabric

There are various types of fur fabric available, with long or short pile, polished or un-polished. Short pile fur fabric is used for the toys in this book unless otherwise stated. If you have difficulty obtaining fur fabric locally see the suppliers list at the end of the book. On these fabrics the fur pile lies smooth and flat if stroked in one direction, and will lift up if stroked in the opposite direction.

On patterns for fur fabric toys, the direction of the 'smooth stroke' of the fur pile is indicated by an arrow on each pattern piece. Always cut the pieces so that the smooth stroke of the fur pile follow the direction of the arrows.

Fleecy fabric is also required for some of the toys. This fabric, sold for making dressing gowns, has a knitted backing and is brushed on the right side to form a soft furry surface. It does not have a pile with a smooth stroke like the other fur fabric.

To cut out fur fabric pieces, pin the patterns, one at a time, to the wrong side of the fabric then snip through the back of the

fabric only, so as not to cut through the fur pile on the right side. When cutting a pair of pieces, always take care to reverse the pattern before cutting the second piece.

To join fur fabric pieces, place the pieces right sides together, tucking in the fur pile at the raw edges, then push in pins at right angles to the raw edges all round, as shown in diagram 3. After sewing, remove all the pins, then turn right side out and pick out all the fur pile trapped in the seam with the point of a pin.

Working with felt

Because felt is a non-woven fabric, it is often supposed that it has no grain. However, it does have varying amounts of stretch when pulled lengthways and sideways as well as stretch across the bias. When using felt for stuffed toys, always cut any identical pieces so that they lie in the same direction, parallel with the selvedge, or a straight edge if a square of felt is being used.

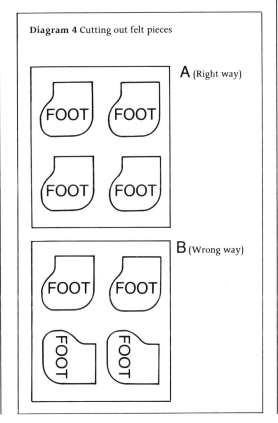

Diagram 4 Cutting out felt pieces

A (Right way)

B (Wrong way)

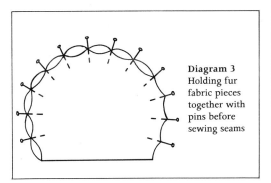

Diagram 3 Holding fur fabric pieces together with pins before sewing seams

Diagram 4a shows an example of the correct way to cut the pieces for a doll's feet. If the feet are cut as shown in diagram 4b there may be differences in size after stuffing due to the felt stretching more in one direction than the other.

Knitting yarn

Where yarn is quoted in the materials for a doll or toy, this means knitting yarn. Most of the dolls in the book have hair made from knitting yarn and it is also used occasionally for working facial features on other toys.

Making rag dolls

Using woven fabrics: Any fine, closely-woven calico, cotton or poly/cotton fabric is suitable for doll-making. While pale pink and peachy shades look nice, cream or white fabric can also be used. If pale pink is difficult to obtain in a dress fabric try to get pink cotton sheeting. Quite a number of shops now have sheeting by the metre for making duvet covers and sheets. It is also worth looking out for sale or bargain offers on poly/cotton sheets in the larger chain stores. If you do a lot of doll-making, a sheet bought in this way can work out cheaper, metre for metre, than buying the fabric.

Always cut out the pieces on the straight grain of the fabric unless the pattern specifies otherwise. Use a small machine stitch for the seams, and trim seams round all curves to about 3 mm ($\frac{1}{8}$ in).

After stuffing, any puckers in the seams can be ironed out as follows. Pinch the toy tightly between finger and thumb to force the stuffing against the puckered seam, then rub the seam against a warm iron.

Using stockinette: Cotton stockinette in flesh or cream colour, is available by the metre specifically for making dolls. If you have difficulty obtaining stockinette, see the suppliers' list on page 139.

Alternatively discarded plain white stockinette vests or T-shirts can be used instead. These can be tinted pink if desired, following the dye-maker's instructions. When dying fabric remember that the colour always looks darker when the fabric is wet. Test a small cutting in the dye solution first.

Although stockinette will stretch in any direction when pulled, it usually stretches most across the width as in hand-knitted fabric. The direction of 'most stretch' is indicated by arrows on each pattern piece or in the instructions, when making dolls from stockinette.

Use a small machine stitch when sewing stockinette, stretching the seams slightly as they are sewn, so that the stitching will not snap when the pieces are stuffed. Trim the seams around all the curves to about 3 mm ($\frac{1}{8}$ in).

For some of the dolls, cuttings off nylon tights or stockings are used for the heads and hands. Stockinette polishing cloth is also required for making three of the dolls. When working with these stretchy materials follow the same procedures as mentioned for cotton stockinette.

Doll's hair

Cutting a number of equal lengths of knitting yarn for a doll's hair is a simple matter if you first wind the yarn into a hank. Select an object of suitable size to wind the yarn around – for example a large book or the back of a chair. Note that the object should be somewhat longer than the required lengths, because the yarn will stretch slightly as it is wound.

After winding your hank, any kinks in the yarn can be removed as follows. Using two wooden spoons or any similar long-handled cooking utensils, slip the handles through each end of the hank. Stretch the hank tightly and steam it by holding it over a pan of boiling water. Finally, cut through the hank at each end.

Colouring cheeks

Use an orange-red pencil for colouring a doll's cheeks and always try the effect on an oddment of fabric first. For woven cotton dolls, gently rub the side of the pencil tip (not the point) over the cheeks. If the colour is too strong or uneven, some of it can be removed by rubbing gently with a soft eraser.

For stockinette dolls, moisten the pencil tip and apply a little colour at the centre of the cheeks. Blend the colour over the cheek area with a bit of damp fabric.

Rosette dolls

The bodies, arms and legs of these dolls are made from fabric circles of different sizes gathered up round the edges then threaded onto lengths of thin cord elastic. This type of elastic, sometimes known as hat elastic, is obtainable in various thicknesses. Elastic of about 2 to 3 mm ($\frac{1}{16}$ to $\frac{1}{8}$ in) in diameter is about the right thickness for the dolls.

You can use any oddments of lightweight plain or printed fabrics for the circles, such as dressmaking leftovers or pieces cut from

Rosette dolls are easy to make and use up any odd scraps of material. See page 100 for the instructions to make these Dutch dolls

discarded garments. If you haven't enough fabric on hand, pay a visit to your local thrift shop or jumble sale where cast off items of clothing can usually be purchased more cheaply than buying fabric by the metre.

The fabric circles can be strung on the lengths of elastic regardless of colour; but to achieve a prettier effect, try grouping similar colours together for each different part of the doll, as shown in the illustrations. Sort your fabrics into piles before cutting out the circles, for example place greens and blues in one pile, reds and oranges in another.

Thin card is required for making the circle templates. You can use card from large breakfast cereal or washing powder packets or any similar grocery packages.

To make the card templates: Draw the circles onto the card with compasses (or string and pencil for larger circles) to the sizes given for each doll. Cut out the card circles then mark the diameter size on each one. Keep all the card circles after making your doll because some of them will come in useful for another doll. To cut out the fabric circles, draw round one of the card templates onto a piece of fabric then cut out the circle. If you need a number of circles of the same size, several can be cut at the same time as follows. Pin the cut-out fabric circle close to the edges all round, onto three or four layers of fabric, then cut through all the fabrics even with the edge of the first circle.

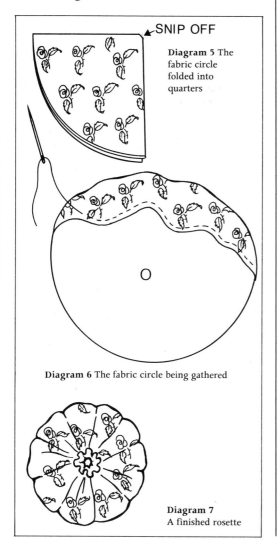

SNIP OFF

Diagram 5 The fabric circle folded into quarters

O

Diagram 6 The fabric circle being gathered

Diagram 7
A finished rosette

To gather the circles: Firstly, fold each circle into quarters then snip off the corner at the centre to make a tiny hole as shown in diagram 5. Run a gathering thread all round about 3 mm ($\frac{1}{8}$ in) from the edge of the circle as shown in diagram 6. Pull up the gathers until the raw edges meet then fasten off. Flatten the gathered circle into a rosette having the gathers lying on top of the centre hole as shown in diagram 7.

Group the same size circles together as you make them and add a paper label to each pile, marked with the letter of the alphabet given for that size of circle in the instructions for each doll.

Stuffing the toy

Various types of filling are available for making toys. Foam chips should not be used as they can be highly flammable. Kapok is quite good, but rather messy to work with as the fibres fly everywhere. Man-made fibre fillings are very clean to work with, and they have the added advantage of being washable. These fillings come in several grades, ranging from luxury high bulk white polyester to inexpensive multi-coloured filling, for use only when the colour will not show through the 'skin' of the toy.

For rag dolls and small- to medium-sized soft toys, the most expensive polyester filling gives a lovely even finish. Since it goes further (due to being high bulk), this filling can be just as economical to use as a cheaper type, where more filling would be needed. For larger items, such as sit-upon toys which need to be firmly stuffed, the cheaper fillings are ideal.

Lumpy toys are usually the result of uneven stuffing, because small gaps are left where one piece of filling ends and the next begins. This generally occurs in narrow pieces such as the limbs of a rag doll. When stuffing these, take a large handful of filling and tease it into an elongated shape. Push one end of the filling right into the end of the limb, then gradually feed in the filling with the fingers, trying to keep it in a continuous piece. Keep feeling the limb as it is stuffed, both inside and outside, taking care to fill any empty areas. When the piece of filling is almost finished, introduce one end of another piece in the same way, so that the fibres of the first piece will blend with the next.

If the limb is too narrow to get a finger inside, push in the filling with the end of a pencil or knob of a knitting needle. To stuff very small toys, use tweezers.

Attaching head or limbs

To hold the head or limb securely to the body while sewing it in place, use a couple of darning needles instead of pins. Push the needles first into the body fabric, then into the head or limb, then back into the body fabric as shown in diagram 8.

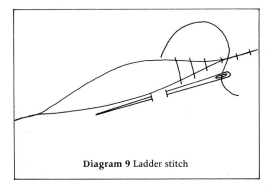

Diagram 9 Ladder stitch

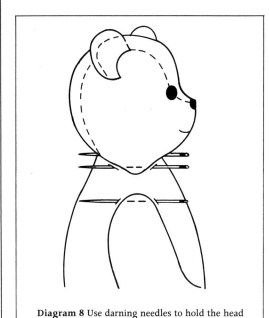

Diagram 8 Use darning needles to hold the head or limb to the body before sewing in place

Ladder stitch

This stitch is used for closing the opening on a soft toy after stuffing. The raw edges of the fabric are turned in at the seam line, then the folded edges are laced together. Use strong double thread and take small, straight stitches alternatively along one side, then the other. After working a few stitches, pull the thread up tight, thus bringing the edges together (see diagram 9). Ladder stitch can also be used to make an invisible join when attaching the head or limb of a toy to the body.

Making a face

The age and character of a doll or animal are mainly determined by the positioning of the facial features. For a child-like appearance, eyes should be placed about half way down the face, not too close together but not too wide apart. For a more grown-up look place the eyes a little higher up and closer together. If measurements are given in the instructions for positioning the facial features, always follow these and your toy should look exactly like the one in the illustration.

If the eyes are made from felt, first pin them to the face, pushing the pins straight through the eyes and into the toy. Now check that they are level and centrally placed on the face by looking at the toy through a mirror. Any irregularities will show up immediately. The same method can be used if eyes and noses are to be embroidered, by pinning small paper shapes to the face before actually marking the fabric. An embroidered mouth line can be marked in the same way using a short length of thick thread or yarn, pinned to the face as a guide.

When embroidering facial features, secure the knotted end of the thread in a place where it will not be seen on the finished toy; for example, at the back of a doll's head or under the position of an eye or nose on an animal. Use a darning needle to take the thread through the toy to the position of the embroidered feature. Work the feature using a small needle, then use the darning needle to take the thread back through the toy as before and fasten off the thread.

When sewing or gluing felt features on a fur fabric toy, snip away the fur pile beneath the felt before fixing it in place.

1
LARGE SOFT TOYS

Teddy Bear · 20

Humpty Dumpty · 23

Puss in Boots · 26

Soulful Hound Dog · 31

Mascot Teddy Bears · 34

Mr and Mrs Bunny · 40

Mother and Baby Panda 45

Mother and Baby Bear 48

Teddy Bear

This traditional Teddy with his jointed arms and legs would make a super raffle prize for your local bazaar or, of course, the perfect gift for a favourite child. He measures 53 cm (21 in) tall

You will need: 50 cm ($\frac{5}{8}$ yd) of fur fabric 138 cm (54 in) wide; 500 g (about 1 lb) of stuffing; four 45 mm ($1\frac{3}{4}$ in) hardboard joints (see supplier's list on page 139); two 15 mm ($\frac{5}{8}$ in) diameter black buttons for eyes (optional); pieces of chamois leather or felt for foot and paw pads; scraps of thick felt, leathercloth or leather for masking the joints; scraps of black and brown felt and black yarn; small round-nosed pliers for bending the cotter pins on joints; metric graph paper; some wide ribbon.

Notes: The seam allowance is 5 mm ($\frac{1}{4}$ in) on all pieces except for paw pads – these are sewn round the edges to completed arms. Join pieces with right sides facing.

Copy the patterns onto metric graph paper, square by square (each square on diagram equals 2 cm).

From the patterns, cut out all pieces from fur fabric except for the foot and paw pads. Cut these from chamois or felt.

Mark the positions for the joints on wrong side of fur fabric.

To insert a joint: Each joint consists of two hardboard discs, two metal washers and a cotter pin. Also required are two circles of thick fabric such as felt or leathercloth cut out about 15 mm ($\frac{5}{8}$ in) larger in diameter than the discs. These are used to mask the hard edges of the joint against the fur fabric body and limbs.

Make up the limb as given in the instructions leaving the top edges open as indicated on the pattern. After stuffing the limb, take a joint set and on to the cotter pin thread a washer then a hardboard disc and lastly a circle of material. Push the cotter pin through the fabric at the marked point on the inside of the limb. Continue stuffing the limb around and above the joint to make it quite firm then ladder stitch the opening at the top of each limb.

Attach the completed limbs to the body,

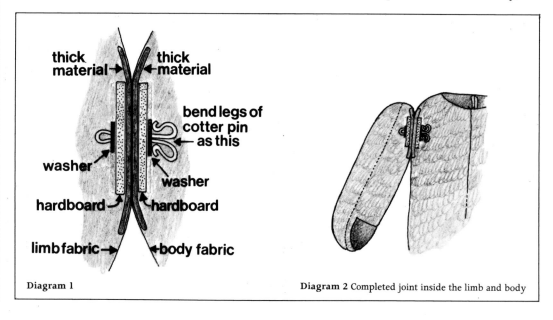

thick material → ← **thick material**

→ **bend legs of cotter pin — as this**

washer →

← **washer**

hardboard → ← **hardboard**

limb fabric → ← **body fabric**

Diagram 1

Diagram 2 Completed joint inside the limb and body

before it is stuffed, as follows. Push the cotter pin protruding from the limb through the marked point on the body fabric then thread on a circle of material, a hardboard disc and, lastly, a washer. Now using the round-nosed pliers and taking each leg of the cotter pin in turn, pull upwards very hard and firmly bend it over into the shape shown in diagram 1 so that the leg is pressing hard against the washer. Diagram 2 shows a completed joint in position inside the limb and body. The joint should be as tight as possible.

After all the limbs are jointed on to the body, the body can be stuffed taking care to pack stuffing very carefully around each of the joints.

The teddy

For the arms: Join the pieces in pairs leaving a gap in the seam at upper edges as indicated. Turn right side out and stuff as far as the opening. Insert a joint on each arm taking care to make a pair. Finish off stuffing arms then ladder stitch the openings. Cut out two paw pads from felt or chamois leather following the dotted line on arm pattern. Stitch a paw pad in position on each arm as shown on arm pattern.

The legs: Join the pieces in pairs leaving the lower edges open and a gap in the seam at the upper edges as indicated on the pattern. Stitch a foot pad to the lower edges of each leg matching points A and B. Turn legs right side out, stuff, insert joints and finish off as for arms.

The body: Join the body pieces leaving the upper neck edges open and a gap in the seam at the back as indicated. Turn the body right side out, push cotter pins on limbs through the marked positions on the body and finish off the jointing on each limb. Stuff the body firmly then ladder stitch the back opening. Continue stuffing the body through the neck opening then run a gathering thread round raw edge of neck. Pull up gathers and fasten off, leaving about a 5 cm (2 in) opening in the neck. Continue stuffing through this opening to shape shoulders above the arms.

The head: Sew gusset to head pieces, matching points C, round top of head to D. Join the centre front seam of head pieces. Turn right side out and stuff very firmly. Run a gathering thread round neck edge, continue stuffing then fasten off thread leaving about a 5 cm (2 in) diameter opening.

Place the head on top of the body matching the centre front and back seams. Using very strong thread, ladder stitch the head to the body all round about 1 cm ($\frac{3}{8}$ in) from the raw edges, pull up thread tightly and make a back stitch every so often to hold the thread taut. Push more stuffing into neck between head and body if necessary to make quite firm before completing ladder stitching. Ladder stitch around the join twice more to make it quite secure.

The ears: Join ear pieces in pairs leaving the lower edges open. Turn right side out, turn in lower raw edges and oversew, pulling up stitches to gather slightly. Pin the ears on the head using the illustration, as a guide, then oversew them in place all round lower edges.

The nose and mouth: Clip the fur fabric short all round snout and mouth area. Using black yarn, work a straight stitch down from point of snout then a V on either side of this as illustrated. Cut a triangle of black felt 2 cm ($\frac{3}{4}$ in) across the base and 1·5 cm ($\frac{5}{8}$ in) at the apex. Sew this in place at end of snout as illustrated.

The eyes: Cut two 2 cm ($\frac{3}{4}$ in) diameter circles of brown felt. Place a button in the centre of each and using very strong thread sew buttons to head through felt circles at positions shown in illustration. The eyes should be set about 5·5 cm ($2\frac{1}{4}$ in) apart and level with the nose. The buttons can be replaced with circles of black felt sewing both circles in place on head.

To complete Teddy, tie a ribbon bow round his neck, trimming the ends of the ribbon into a V-shape for a smart finish.

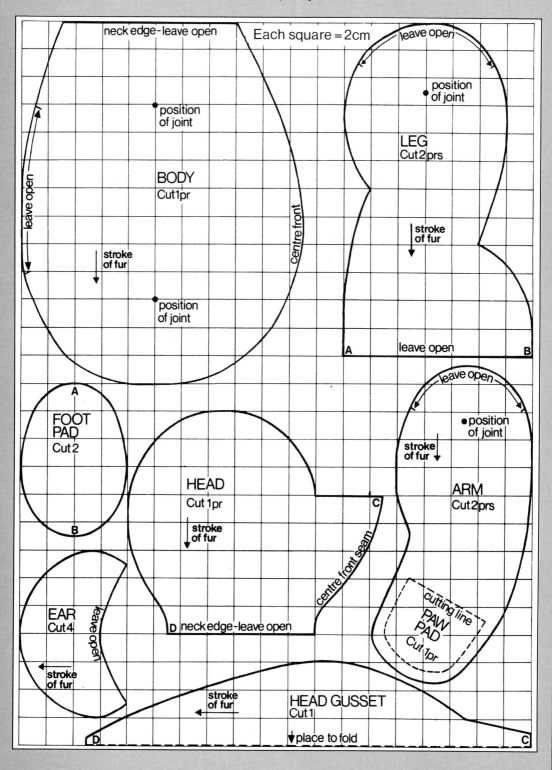

Each square = 2cm

neck edge-leave open

leave open

LEG
Cut 2 prs

• position of joint

stroke of fur

leave open

• position of joint

BODY
Cut 1 pr

stroke of fur

Centre front

• position of joint

A | leave open | B

FOOT PAD
Cut 2

A

B

leave open

HEAD
Cut 1 pr

• position of joint

stroke of fur

ARM
Cut 2 prs

C

centre front seam

cutting line

PAW PAD
Cut 1 pr

EAR
Cut 4

leave open

stroke of fur

D | neck edge-leave open

stroke of fur

stroke of fur

HEAD GUSSET
Cut 1

D ↓ place to fold C

Humpty Dumpty

This super-sized Humpty Dumpty measures roughly 51 cm (20 in) from top to toe. He can be made mostly from oddments, but it is best to use firm, closely-woven fabrics for the upper and lower body pieces

You will need: 40 cm ($\frac{1}{2}$ yd) of 91 cm (36 in) wide fabric for upper body and hands; 20 cm ($\frac{1}{4}$ yd) of 91 cm (36 in) wide fabric for lower body; oddments of fabric for circles to make arms and legs; oddments of fabric and narrow ribbon for feet; 500 g (1 lb) of stuffing; small ball of thick yarn for hair; 40 cm ($\frac{1}{2}$ yd) of 91 cm (36 in) wide fabric for cap; scraps of felt and black embroidery thread for facial features; 2 m ($2\frac{1}{4}$ yd) of strong cotton tape for threading arm and leg circles; 80 cm ($\frac{7}{8}$ yd) of braid or ribbon for belt; ribbon scrap for bow at front; adhesive; metric graph paper.

Notes: Copy the patterns, square by square, on to metric graph paper (each square on diagram equals 2 cm). Take special care to copy the body pieces as accurately as possible, to get an egg-shaped toy.

The seam allowance is 1 cm ($\frac{3}{8}$ in) on all pieces unless otherwise stated. Join all fabrics with right sides facing.

Humpty Dumpty

For body: Cut four upper and four lower body pieces from appropriate fabrics.

Sew two lower body pieces to two upper body pieces, along straight edges. Then join these entire body lengths together at one side edge, to complete the back of toy.

For arm tapes: Cut two 40 cm ($15\frac{3}{4}$ in) lengths of tape. Take the two remaining lower body pieces for fronts, fold tapes in half and stitch folded ends to right side of fabric at positions shown on lower body pattern, taking care to place them so that there is one left and one right arm tape (see diagram 1).

For leg tapes: Cut two 60 cm ($23\frac{1}{2}$ in) lengths of tape. Fold each tape in half. Cut a small slit in each lower front body piece where shown on pattern, then slip the folded end of each leg tape through the slit (see diagram 2). Fold and sew fabric together at dotted line positions, forming darts to hold tapes in place, then sew again within dart stitching to reinforce. Join lower body pieces to the two remaining upper body pieces, then join these entire pieces at one side edge, making sure that arm tapes are correctly positioned to come at each side of the toy.

Now join back portion to the front, taking care not to catch tapes in seam and leaving a gap in seam at top of toy for stuffing. Turn

right side out, stuff very firmly, then ladder stitch opening.

For face : Cut two eyes, two pupils and nose from felt, using the patterns. Position lower edge of nose 8 cm (3 in) above the body seam line, then stick it in place. Glue pupils to eyes then stick eyes slightly above level of nose and 2·5 cm (1 in) apart.

Work a curved line for mouth, 4 cm (1½ in) below nose, in back stitch using black embroidery thread. Work back along mouth line, oversewing through each back stitch. Cut two 6 cm (2⅜ in) diameter circles of felt for cheeks and glue in place as shown in illustration.

For hair : Wind a yarn strand five times round four fingers. Slip this small hank off fingers and machine stitch through one end of loops. Continue winding yarn round fingers and stitching loops until you've made a looped fringe 30 cm (12 in) long. Sew stitched ends of loops to front of forehead at dotted line position on upper body.

Sew a strip of ribbon or braid round centre seam of toy, then sew a ribbon bow to the centre front.

For hands : Cut two pairs of hand pieces. Join them in pairs, leaving upper edges open. Clip seam all round and at thumb, as shown on pattern. Turn right side out and stuff, then put the hands aside.

For feet : Cut two pairs of foot pieces; make up as for hands and put them aside.

The arms and legs

For the circles : Cut an 18 cm (7 in) diameter circle of card to use as a template for the leg circles, and a 16 cm (6¼ in) diameter card circle for arm circles. Draw round the templates on to fabric then cut out the circles.

Cut twenty circles for each leg, and ten circles for each arm and snip a small hole in the centre of each. Run a gathering thread round edge of each circle. Pull up gathers until raw edges touch, fasten off.

For each ankle frill cut a fabric strip 9 by 38 cm (3½ by 15 in). Join short edges then fold in half lengthways with right side outside

bringing raw edges together. Run a gathering thread round raw edges, pull up tightly, fasten off.

For each wrist frill cut a fabric strip 8 by 32 cm (3 by 12½ in). Make as for ankle frills.

To assemble each arm : Thread ten circles and wrist frill on doubled arm tape. Knot tape ends several times close to the wrist frill. Now push the arm circles back up the arm tape towards the body and put a pin through the tape to prevent circles slipping back down the tape. (This will give more room to work when sewing the knotted tape ends inside the hand.) Run a strong gathering thread round upper edge of hand, turn in raw edges and push the knotted tape ends inside hand. Pull up gathers tightly round tape and fasten off. Sew tape securely to hand fabric, through tape and hand.

To assemble each leg : Thread twenty circles and an ankle frill on to one leg tape, and complete as for arm. Sew small bow to foot.

The cap

For top of cap cut a 36 cm (14 in) diameter fabric circle. Mark the centre on right side of fabric to show position of bobble.

For cap band cut a 6 by 60 cm (2⅜ by 23½ in) fabric strip (join strips if necessary to make up the length). Join short edges of the band then fold it in half, right side out, bringing raw edges together. Tack raw edges together all round. Gather outer edge of top of cap to fit band, then join raw edges of band to gathered edge. Turn right side out.

Cut two cap peak pieces and join them along outer edge. Trim seam, turn right side out then stitch through seam at outer edge. Tack inner edge of peak 1 cm (⅜ in) inside cap band, then stitch all round edge of cap band, catching peak in place.

Put cap on Humpty's head, tilting it a little to one side. Slip stitch lower edge of cap band to head all round.

For cap bobble cut a 10 cm (4 in) diameter fabric circle. Gather round edge, stuff centre, pull up gathers, fasten off. Pull top of cap slightly to one side and sew bobble to cap and head at marked centre position.

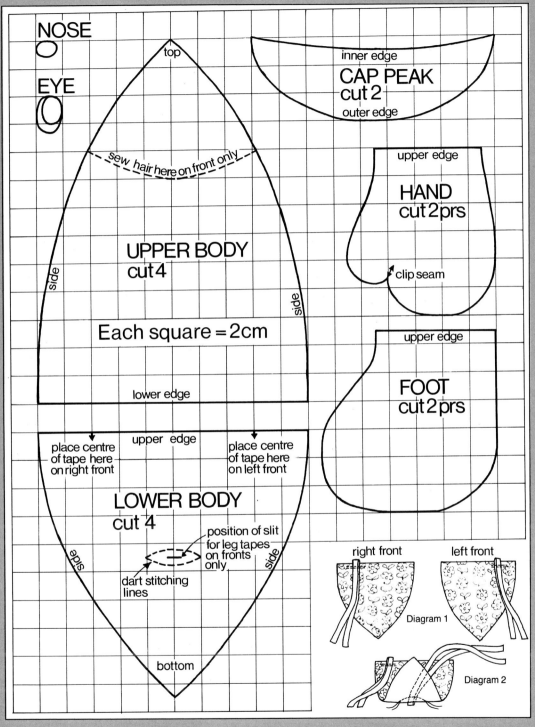

NOSE

EYE

top

sew hair here on front only

side

side

UPPER BODY
cut 4

Each square = 2cm

lower edge

place centre
of tape here
on right front

upper edge

place centre
of tape here
on left front

LOWER BODY
cut 4

side

position of slit
for leg tapes
on fronts
only

dart stitching
lines

side

bottom

CAP PEAK
cut 2

inner edge

outer edge

HAND
cut 2 prs

upper edge

clip seam

FOOT
cut 2 prs

upper edge

right front

left front

Diagram 1

Diagram 2

Diagram 1 How to sew arm tapes
to lower body pieces
Diagram 2 Folded end of leg tape
pushed through slit, and dart stitched

Puss in Boots

This favourite character from nursery tale and pantomime comes to life as a cuddly toy. He stands about 61 cm (24 in) high in his boots. These are stitched in place to form part of the toy and in addition you can make a complete outfit of clothes; all of which can be removed

Puss in his boots

You will need: For Puss: 40 cm ($\frac{1}{2}$ yd) of fur
fabric 138 cm (54 in) wide; 500 g (1 lb) of
stuffing; scraps of pink black and blue felt;
black 4-ply yarn and white thread.
For his boots: a 46 cm (18 in) square of felt;
small pieces of strong card and black felt;
two small buckles; 80 cm ($\frac{7}{8}$ yd) of braid
for boot tops; 80 cm ($\frac{7}{8}$ yd) of broad bootlace;
adhesive; a sheet of metric graph paper at
least 46 by 60 cm (18 by 23 in).
Notes: The seam allowance is 1 cm ($\frac{3}{8}$ in)

On metric graph paper draw out all outlines
and markings from diagram square by square
(each square on diagram equals 2 cm). To get
complete pattern for body, trace the full-size
pattern off your graph paper on to folded
tracing paper, placing the fold in tracing
paper against fold line marked on pattern.

Cut out your patterns and pin them to the
wrong side of fur fabric, then cut out pieces
as shown in diagram 1, also cutting a strip 10
by 40 cm (4 by 15$\frac{3}{4}$ in) for tail. Transfer all
markings onto the wrong side of the fur fabric.

Join seams with right sides of fabric facing
unless otherwise stated.

Puss

Join body pieces round edges, leaving a gap
in seam, and leaving lower leg edges open as
shown on pattern. Machine along stitching
lines between legs, then cut fabric open as on
pattern. Clip seam at neck then turn right
side out.

Stuff head and body firmly through side
opening, then slip stitch this opening.
Continue stuffing through lower leg edges. Tie
strong thread very tightly round neck and
sew thread ends into body.

Join ear pieces in pairs, leaving lower
edges open as on pattern. Trim off points and
turn right side out. Turn in lower edges 1 cm
($\frac{3}{8}$ in) and oversew them together, pulling
stitches tight to gather slightly. Sew ears in
place as shown on pattern.

Join long edges of tail strip, tapering
slightly towards one end then rounding off
seam across this end. Trim seam and turn tail
right side out, using a thick knitting needle
to do this easily. Stuff the tail very lightly,

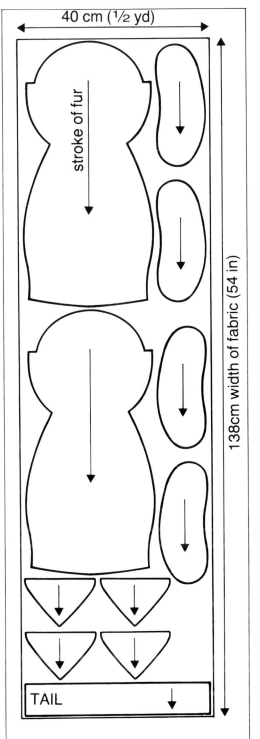

Diagram 1 How to cut fur fabric pieces – arrows
show the horizontal stroke of the pile

pushing in small amounts of stuffing with knitting needle. Turn in remaining raw edge and slip stitch it to back of Puss as shown on the pattern.

Join arm pieces in pairs, leaving gaps in seams at top, as on pattern. Trim seams round paws and turn right side out. Stuff arms firmly to about halfway up, then stuff very lightly. Turn in and slip stitch raw edges, then sew tops of arms to Puss (see pattern).

Following pattern cut two oval eye shapes in blue felt, and two circles of black felt; glue them together in pairs. Using white thread work a highlight on each eye as shown in illustration. Cut nose from pink felt.

Carefully clip fur fabric a bit shorter at centre of face around mouth and nose area. Position eyes and nose on face with pins, using illustration as a guide.

With black yarn, work a stitch straight down from nose, then back-stitch remaining mouth lines, oversewing through each back stitch. Work whiskers with long straight stitches. Glue on eyes and nose, holding them in place with pins until glue dries.

Boots

Cut four uppers from felt. Join centre front and back seam. Trim seams and turn right side out. Cut two card soles and place one inside each boot at lower edge. Glue lower edges of boots 1 cm ($\frac{3}{8}$ in) onto soles all round, matching points A and B. Stuff boots very firmly. Cut two black felt soles and stick them over card soles. Glue strips of bootlace round lower edges of boots, as shown in illustration.

Cut two boot top pieces from folded felt, placing edge marked fold against fold in felt. Sew fancy braid to outer edge of each piece, then join short edges taking a tiny seam. Slip a boot top piece over each leg of Puss, with wrong sides out and braid edges uppermost. Pin the boots to the lower edges of legs, with the felt overlapping the fur fabric by 1 cm ($\frac{3}{8}$ in), and turning toes of boots outwards slightly. Slip stitch top edges of boots to legs as pinned, adding more stuffing as necessary to make legs and boots quite firm.

Bring inner edges of boot tops to top edges of boots and oversew them in place, matching centre back seams. Then turn top pieces

down over boots. Sew centre bar of each buckle to a boot front. Cut two buckle flaps from felt and thread one through each buckle, holding it in place with a few stitches.

Shirt

You will need: 40 cm ($\frac{1}{2}$ yd) of 91 cm (36 in) wide fabric; three small buttons; 140 cm ($1\frac{1}{2}$ yd) of lace edging, 6 cm ($2\frac{3}{8}$ in) wide.

To make: Cut two shirt pieces, placing edge marked fold to fold in fabric. Cut one piece open along fold line for centre front of shirt (the other piece will be the shirt back).

Trace sleeve pattern off shirt pattern, then cut two sleeves, placing edge marked fold to fold in fabric. Join one armhole edge of each sleeve to armhole edge of shirt back. Join remaining armhole edge of sleeve to armhole edge of each shirt front. Clip curves in seams and press seams towards sleeves.

Hem each lower sleeve edge then sew on a 40 cm ($15\frac{3}{4}$ in) strip of lace edging gathered to fit. Join entire side and underarm seams of shirt, including lace edging. Hem the lower edge of the shirt.

Turn in centre front edges 2 cm ($\frac{3}{4}$ in) and press. Turn in raw edges of these turnings and stitch them down.

Neaten the cut ends of remaining lace edging and sew it round neck edge of shirt, missing the turned-in edges at centre front. Gather neck edge all round to fit Puss's neck, leaving the turn-in edges at centre front ungathered. Bind neck edge with bias strip of fabric. Sew buttons to right front edge, and make buttonholes in left front.

Breeches

You will need: 30 cm ($\frac{3}{8}$ yd) of 91 cm (36 in) wide fabric; 80 cm ($\frac{7}{8}$ yd) narrow elastic.

To make: Cut two breeches pieces, placing fold line on pattern to fold in fabric. Join the pieces at centre edges, leaving a gap for tail in one seam as shown on pattern. Clip seams at curves and press open. Turn in and slip stitch raw edges at gap in seam, then join inside leg edges.

Turn in waist and lower edges 5 mm then 1 cm ($\frac{1}{4}$ in then $\frac{3}{8}$ in), and stitch to form casings for elastic. Thread through elastic to fit waist and legs.

Belt

You need: A buckle; a strip of leather cloth or felt about 70 cm ($\frac{3}{4}$ yd) long, and wide enough to fit the centre bar of buckle.

To make: Attach one end of belt strip to centre bar of buckle, cutting a hole to fit over centre prong. Round off other end, then cut more small holes along centre of belt.

Cape

You will need: 30 cm by 60 cm (12 in by 24 in) of velvet and of lining fabric; 120 cm ($1\frac{3}{8}$ yd) of ric-rac or braid; 50 cm ($\frac{1}{2}$ yd) of narrow ribbon.

To make: For a pattern draw out a 58 cm (23 in) diameter semi-circle on paper then draw and cut out a 20 cm (8 in) diameter semi-circle at centre of straight edge for neck edge. Using the pattern cut cape from velvet and lining fabric.

Join both pieces round edges, leaving a gap in neck edge seam for turning. Trim the seam all round, turn right side out and press cape. Turn in and slip stitch gap.

Cut the ribbon in two and sew half to each end of neck seam, for ties. Sew ric-rac braid round close to the edges of the cape, as illustrated.

Hat

You will need: 50 cm ($\frac{1}{2}$ yd) of 91 cm (36 in) wide felt (or three 46 cm (18 in) squares); a 34 cm ($13\frac{1}{2}$ in) square of stiff interlining; 50 cm ($\frac{1}{2}$ yd) of braid for hatband; a few feathers; a large button; adhesive.

To make: For a hat brim pattern draw out a 34 cm ($13\frac{1}{2}$ in) diameter circle with a 12 cm ($4\frac{3}{4}$ in) diameter circle cut out of centre. Cut two of these shapes from felt.

From interlining cut a 33 cm (13 in) diameter circle with a 14 cm ($5\frac{1}{2}$ in) diameter circle cut out of centre. Spread glue round edges of interlining and stick it centrally over one felt piece. Stick the other felt piece on top

in the same way, sandwiching interlining between felt circles.

Stitch felt brim pieces together round outer edges, then stitch inner edges together 1 cm ($\frac{3}{8}$ in) from raw edges of felt. Clip inner edges all round, back to stitching.

For crown of hat cut a felt strip 44 cm by 16 cm ($17\frac{1}{2}$ in by $6\frac{1}{4}$ in). Join short edges, taking 5 mm ($\frac{1}{4}$ in) seam. Press seam open.

Slip one end of this tube, wrong side out, inside the centre hole of brim, with raw edges of felt level. Pin in place, then back stitch brim and crown together through stitching line all round, as shown in diagram 2. Trim seam then push the tube up through brim to turn it right side out. Note that the trimmed raw edges of back-stitched seam are now on the outside. Oversew these raw edges to crown, then cover them with braid.

Gather tightly all round top edge of crown and fasten off. Cover gathered edges with a felt-covered button. Sew feathers to hat.

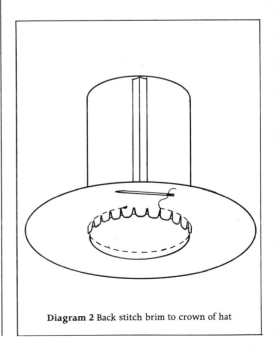

Diagram 2 Back stitch brim to crown of hat

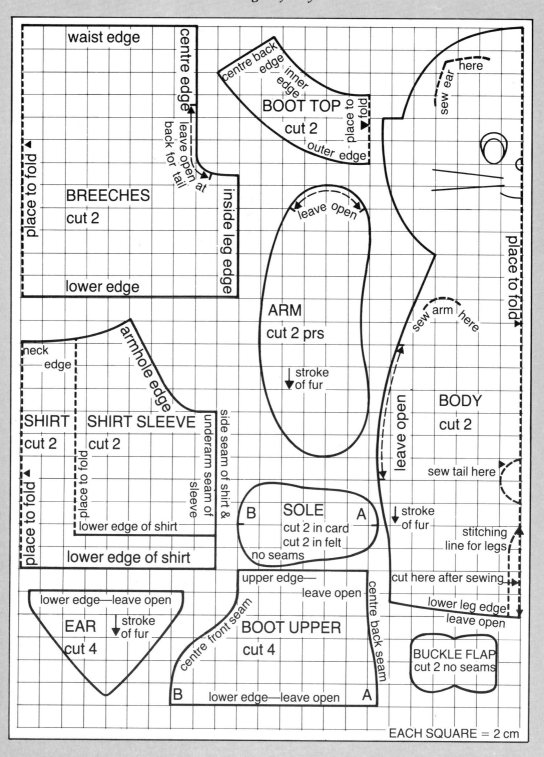

waist edge

centre edge

BOOT TOP
cut 2

centre back edge

inner edge

place to fold

outer edge

sew ear here

leave open at back for tail

BREECHES
cut 2

place to fold

inside leg edge

place to fold

leave open

ARM
cut 2 prs

stroke of fur

sew arm here

BODY
cut 2

leave open

neck edge

armhole edge

SHIRT
cut 2

SHIRT SLEEVE
cut 2

place to fold

underarm seam of sleeve

side seam of shirt & sleeve

lower edge of shirt

place to fold

lower edge of shirt

B

SOLE
cut 2 in card
cut 2 in felt
no seams

A

sew tail here

stroke of fur

stitching line for legs

cut here after sewing

lower leg edge
leave open

lower edge—leave open

EAR
cut 4

stroke of fur

upper edge—
leave open

centre front seam

BOOT UPPER
cut 4

centre back seam

BUCKLE FLAP
cut 2 no seams

B

lower edge—leave open

A

EACH SQUARE = 2 cm

Soulful Hound Dog

This lovable hound dog with his long droopy ears and doleful expression makes a cuddly bedtime toy for toddlers or an endearing mascot for the young at heart. He is 53 cm (21 in) long, from the tip of his nose to his tail

You will need: 50 cm ($\frac{5}{8}$ yd) of 138 cm (54 in) wide fur fabric; small pieces of light coloured fur fabric for ear linings; 500 g (1 lb) of stuffing; scraps of pink, black and blue felt for eyes; small piece of shiny fabric such as taffeta for nose; 1 m (1$\frac{1}{8}$ yd) of ribbon or braid.

Notes: Join all fur fabric pieces with right sides facing and taking 5 mm ($\frac{1}{4}$ in) seams.

Using the diagram draw out all the pattern pieces square by square onto metric graph paper (each square on diagram equals 5 cm). Transfer all markings on to each piece.

Cut out all the fur fabric pieces with the smooth stroke of the pile in the direction indicated by the arrows on the patterns. The body gusset should be cut out across the width of the fabric disregarding the direction of the pile.

The dog

Cut out one pair of body pieces, marking points A, B, C, D and E, then join them along their top edges from point A to point E. Cut gusset and mark all points as for body. Stitch gusset to body matching all marked points and leaving a gap in one seam between points C and D. Turn right side out, stuff firmly then ladder stitch the opening.

Cut out four foot pieces and join them in pairs leaving back edges open. Turn right side out and stuff. Turn in raw edges and slip stitch to close. Place feet side by side under dog so back edges of feet are about 36 cm (14 in) from point E. Ladder stitch feet to gusset and body where they touch.

Cut out one pair of tail pieces and join them leaving straight edge open. Turn right side out, stuff firmly, then turn in raw edges and ladder stitch to gusset about 15 cm (6 in) down from point E.

Cut out two ears and two ear linings. Join them in pairs, easing ears to fit linings and leaving top edges open. Turn right side out then turn in raw edges and slip stitch, pulling up stitches to gather slightly. Sew ears to top of head at positions shown on pattern.

Cut two eyes from blue felt, two eyelids from pink felt and two pupils from black felt. Sew pupils to eyes then sew on eyelids, with

their lower edges overlapping top edges of eyes by 5 mm ($\frac{1}{4}$ in). Sew eyes in position on head about 1 cm ($\frac{3}{8}$ in) apart, 2 cm ($\frac{3}{4}$ in) below ears.

For the mouth, cut a 5 mm by 9 cm ($\frac{1}{4}$ in by 3$\frac{1}{2}$ in) strip of black felt. Sew the strip to centre of gusset, starting about 8 cm (3$\frac{1}{8}$ in) below eyes and making a curved line as shown in illustration. You may need to trim the fur pile around the mouth strip. At the lower end of mouth, sew a 5 mm by 3 cm ($\frac{1}{4}$ in by 1$\frac{1}{4}$ in) strip of black felt. For eyebrows cut two 5 mm by 2 cm ($\frac{1}{4}$ in by $\frac{3}{4}$ in) strips of black felt and sew one above each eye.

Cut six 5 mm by 4 cm ($\frac{1}{4}$ in by 1$\frac{1}{2}$ in) strips of black felt and sew three to each foot to mark toes as shown in illustration.

From taffeta, cut one nose piece. Bring curved edges together and join along stitching lines as indicated by dotted lines on the pattern. Run a gathering thread round raw edge of nose and stuff very firmly, pulling up gathers until raw edges touch. Ladder stitch nose in position, slightly overlapping the top end of mouth strip. Tie ribbon round neck.

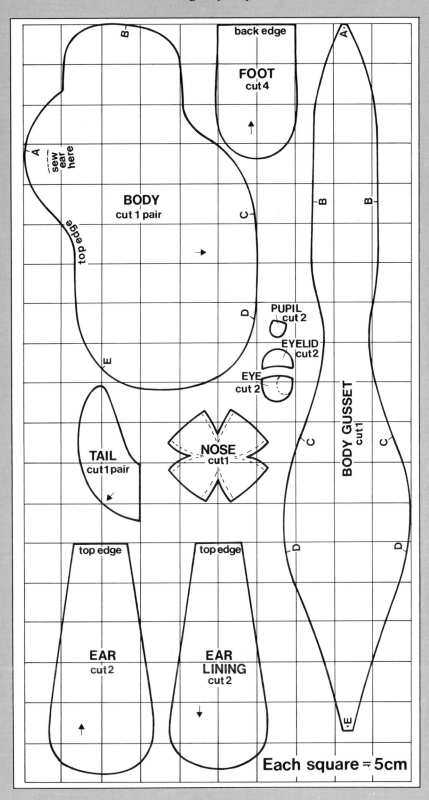

FOOT
cut 4

back edge

A

sew
ear
here

BODY
cut 1 pair

top edge

A

B

B

B

C

D

E

PUPIL
cut 2

EYELID
cut 2

EYE
cut 2

BODY GUSSET
cut 1

C

C

TAIL
cut 1 pair

NOSE
cut 1

D

D

top edge

top edge

EAR
cut 2

EAR
LINING
cut 2

E

Each square = 5cm

Mascot Teddy Bears

Twinkletoes Ted is a football mascot who can be kitted out in the strip of your favourite club team. The same basic pattern will also make up Superbear, a tubby teddy clad in leotard, mask and glittering cape. Both bears measure 48 cm (19 in) in height

For each bear you will need: 45 cm ($\frac{1}{2}$ yd) of 138 cm (54 in) wide fur fabric; 600 g ($1\frac{1}{4}$ lb) of stuffing; scraps of black, white, and brown felt and white thread; metric graph paper; adhesive.

Notes: On to 5 cm squared graph paper copy the pattern shapes, following the outlines on diagram square by square. For the head gusset and the mask patterns, trace the full-size patterns on to folded paper, placing the folded edge at the positions indicated on the patterns. Cut out, then open up the tracings to make whole pattern pieces.

The seam allowance is 5 mm ($\frac{1}{4}$ in) on all Teddy and garment pattern pieces unless otherwise stated.

When sewing seams on stretchy fabric, stretch the fabric slightly while stitching.

The Teddy Bear

Cut two pairs of arm pieces and join them in pairs leaving the top edges open. Turn right side out and stuff to within 3 cm ($1\frac{1}{4}$ in) of the top, then pin fur fabric here to hold stuffing in place. Tack top raw edges of each arm together.

Cut one pair of fronts and one pair of backs and join them in pairs at centre front and centre back edges from neck edge to points A. Now tack the top edges of the arms to the right side of body back pieces at positions shown on the pattern, with raw edges level and the arms pointing inwards.

Make sure also to have the curves of the arms pointing towards the neck edge.

Now tack the front body to the back at side edges and round the legs and feet to points A. Stitch the seams as tacked, then turn the body right side out. Remove the pins in the arms.

Stuff the legs and body, then run a strong gathering thread round neck edge, pull up the gathers to close completely then fasten off.

Cut one pair of head pieces and one head gusset. Sew the side dart in each head piece. Join the head pieces at the centre front, from point A to the neck edge. Insert the gusset, matching points A and B on the head and gusset pieces. Turn the head right side out, stuff, then gather the neck as for the body.

Place the head on top of the body, matching the gathered portions. Hold the head in place with three or four darning needles pushed into the head and body fabric. Ladder-stitch head and body together where they touch, using strong thread. Trim the fur fabric pile slightly shorter on the face below point A.

Cut the eye pieces from felt as follows – cut smallest ovals in black, medium ovals in brown and largest ovals in white. Glue eye pieces together as shown on the pattern then use white thread to work a highlight on each black oval as shown in illustration. Place the eyes in position (see illustration), about 4 cm ($1\frac{1}{2}$ in) apart. Trim away the fur pile underneath each eye then stick them in place and sew them securely round the edges.

Cut two nose pieces from black felt. Oversew them together all round the edges, but before completing the sewing push in a little stuffing. Sew the nose to the end of snout.

For the mouth cut a 5 mm by 8 cm ($\frac{1}{4}$ by 3 in) strip of black felt. Pin the strip in place, then sew it in position using back stitches. Trim off any fur pile which overlaps the mouth strip.

For eyebrows cut two 5 mm by 1·5 cm ($\frac{1}{4}$ by $\frac{5}{8}$ in) strips of black felt. Back stitch them in place above the eyes.

Cut four ear pieces and join them in pairs, leaving lower edges open. Turn them right side out and oversew the lower edges of each ear together, pulling the stitches to gather slightly. Sew ears to top of head, placing them about 8 cm (3 in) apart.

Clothes for Twinkletoes Ted

You will need: For the football shirt, pieces of stretchy fabric (from an old T-shirt, sweater or jersey dress); for the shorts, 20 cm ($\frac{1}{4}$ yd) of 91 cm (36 in) wide nylon or cotton fabric and a short length of elastic; for the socks, cuttings off a pair of old socks; for the boots, small pieces of black felt, 1·30 m ($1\frac{3}{8}$ yd) of 13 mm ($\frac{1}{2}$ in) wide white tape and a short length of sports laces.

Notes: The football strip should be suited to your chosen individual club. Any stripes to go on sleeves, body or shorts pieces should be stitched in place before sewing the pieces together.

To make the shorts: Cut two shorts pieces, placing the pattern to a fold in the fabric each time, as indicated. Hem the leg edges taking narrow turnings. Join the pieces to each other at the centre edges then clip the curves in seams. Bring centre seams together then join inside leg edges.

Take 1 cm ($\frac{3}{8}$ in) turnings twice on the waist edge, then thread elastic through to fit waist and join the ends.

To make the shirt: Cut front and back, placing pattern to a fold in the fabric each time as indicated and cutting neck edges as shown on pattern.

For neck bindings cut 3 cm ($1\frac{1}{4}$ in) wide strips of fabric. Mitre the strips for the front V-point, then sew to wrong side of neck edge, turn to the right side and press. Turn in the remaining raw edge of the binding and stitch down. Bind back neck edge in the same way, easing strip to fit curved neckline.

Join the front to the back at shoulder edges. Cut two sleeves and two cuff pieces, placing patterns to fold in fabric as shown on pattern. Join the edge of the cuff marked A-B to edge of sleeve marked A-B, with right sides facing and raw edges level.

Join armhole edges of sleeves to the armhole edges of shirt. Now join sides of shirt and underarm edges of sleeves and cuffs. Turn cuffs to inside and slip stitch the raw edge in place over the seam. Turn in lower raw edge of shirt and sew in place.

Cut two collar pieces, placing pattern to a fold in fabric as shown on pattern. Join the pieces round the edges, leaving a gap in the neck edge. Clip curves in neck edge then turn right side out, press, and slip stitch gap. Stitch all round outer edge of the collar. Slip stitch neck edge of collar to neck edge of shirt.

To make the socks: Use the leg portion of the socks only and also cut off any elasticated portion at the top. A 12 cm ($4\frac{3}{4}$ in) length is about right. Machine stitch round the cut edges of the sock, stretching the sock as it is stitched to prevent laddering. Slip a sock on each leg, with lower raw edge at approximate position of dotted line shown on body front and back patterns. Slip stitch lower edges in place, then roll down tops of socks as illustrated.

To make the boots: Cut four boot pieces from black felt. Fold tape in half along its length and press. Stitch three strips of tape to each boot piece (see pattern) taking care to make pairs.

Join the pieces in pairs at back edges for about 3 cm ($1\frac{1}{4}$ in), then bind the upper edges with tape. Join boot pieces round edges, leaving upper edges open. Turn right side out. Push a little stuffing in toes and heels, then put boots on feet and slip stitch the upper edges to socks. Make two bootlace bows and sew one to the front of each boot.

Clothes for Superbear

You will need: Pieces of stretchy fabric for the leotard (cuttings off an old T-shirt, sweater or jersey dress); small pieces of felt for the belt, buckle, mask, lightning motif and wristbands; 60 cm ($\frac{5}{8}$ yd) of 91 cm (36 in) wide shiny fabric for the cape; 1·50 m ($1\frac{5}{8}$ yd) of silver braid or trimming; four gold or silver buttons with shanks (or circles of felt if the mascot is for a young child); adhesive.

To make the leotard: Make the patterns from the front and back body patterns, trimming the lower edges along the dotted lines shown on the patterns. Cut one pair of fronts and one pair of backs. Join them in pairs at centre front and centre back edges, from neck to points A. Join the front and back pieces at the sides, from leg edge to points B. Turn in the remainder of the side edges and slip stitch in place. Bring the centre front and back seams together then join the inner leg edges from points A to C.

Turn right side out and put leotard on the bear. Turn in neck edge as necessary to fit close to the neck, then catch the neck and side edges together at each side above the arms. Catch the neck edge to the neck all round with large, loose stitches.

Turn in the leg edges as necessary to fit, then slip stitch them to the legs all round.

To make the belt: Cut a 4 cm ($1\frac{1}{2}$ in) wide strip of felt, long enough to go round the body (about 52 cm, or $20\frac{1}{2}$ in). Stitch the braid to the long edges of the belt. Place the belt on the bear and join the short ends at front, then sew the belt to the leotard.

Cut the buckle from two layers of felt glued together. Stitch all round the edge. Pierce four holes at positions shown on the pattern and push the button shanks through the holes. Sew the buttons to the felt at the back of the buckle, then catch each button to front of belt to hold it in place or sew on felt circles.

To make the lightning motif: Use the pattern to cut the shape from felt. Work lines of stitching on the felt as shown in illustration. Glue the motif in place on the leotard then slip stitch it in place all round the edges.

To make the mask: Cut the mask from two layers of felt glued together. Mark on the eye openings and cut them out using sharp scissors. Stitch all round the edge of the mask. Place it on the bear (see illustration), then glue the portion between and around the eyes in place. With a few stitches, catch the back of the mask to the head at the position of the crosses on pattern.

To make the cape: Make the cape pattern by drawing a 54 cm (21¼ in) diameter semi-circle with a 10 cm (4 in) diameter semi-circle at centre of the straight edge.

Cut two cape pieces from this pattern and join them round the edges, leaving a gap in one straight edge. Turn right side out, press, then slip stitch the gap. Place cape round bear's neck and catch it to the shoulders at each side.

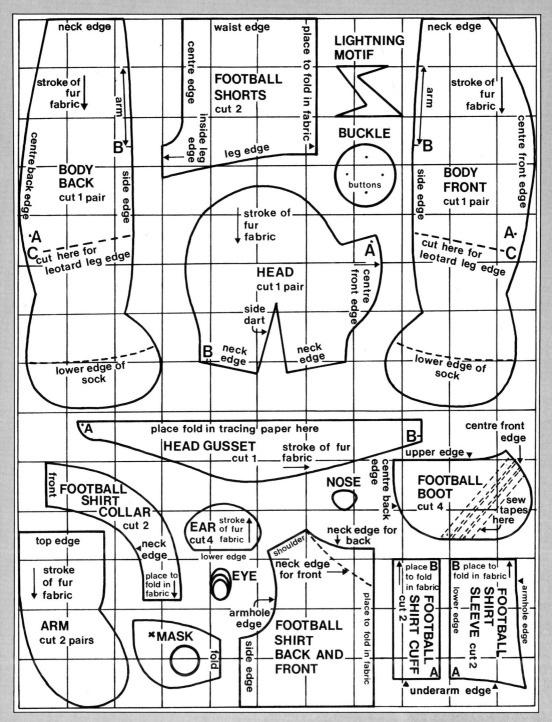

Each square = 5 cm

Mr and Mrs Bunny

They're the best-dressed rabbits around – dandified Mr Bunny, in top hat, tail-frocked coat, waistcoat (with floppy cravat) and trousers; and his elegant partner, dressed up to the nines in Easter bonnet, prettily trimmed dress, petticoat and pantaloons. Each bunny measures about 46 cm (18 in) high

For each bunny you need: 25 cm ($\frac{3}{8}$ yd) of 138 cm (54 in) wide fur fabric; 250 g ($\frac{1}{2}$ lb) of stuffing; scraps of black, brown and white felt, and brown yarn for mouth; scraps of white fleece or felt for ear linings and tail; metric graph paper; adhesive.

Notes: Copy the patterns on to metric graph paper (each square on diagram equals 2 cm).

Cut out all bunny pieces as directed on patterns.

A seam allowance of 5 mm ($\frac{1}{4}$ in) is allowed on all pieces. Join all pieces with right sides facing.

Mark point A on each side head piece. Take a length of coloured thread through to right side of fur fabric to mark position of the dot on each side head piece.

The bunny

Join leg pieces in pairs, leaving the top edges open. Turn right side out and stuff almost to the top. Bring seams together and stitch across tops close to raw edges.

Take one body piece and sew tops of legs to lower edges, where shown on the body pattern, with right sides facing and raw edges level. Let the legs flop down below the body, then join both body pieces round edges, leaving lower edges open and a gap in seam at side, where shown on pattern. Turn body right side out, turn in and slip stitch remaining lower raw edge over seam at tops of legs. Stuff body very firmly through gap in seam, then ladder stitch gap.

Join side head pieces from point A to neck edge. Insert the gusset in top of head, matching points A and B. Turn the head right side out and stuff firmly. Run a strong gathering thread round, 1 cm ($\frac{3}{8}$ in) from neck edge. Pull up gathers as tightly as possible and fasten off. Position this gathered portion of head centrally on top of the body then ladder stitch head to body, working round a few times to secure.

Thread a needle with strong doubled thread and take it through front of face, from the position of one coloured thread to the other. Take thread back through again, about 5 mm ($\frac{1}{4}$ in) above the first stitch, then knot thread ends pulling very tightly. If the fur pile is fairly long, trim it slightly round face area before working facial features, as described below.

For each eye cut a 1·5 cm ($\frac{5}{8}$ in) diameter circle of brown felt. Stick eyes on to slightly larger ovals of white felt. Work a white high-light on each eye. Position eyes on face, at each side of coloured threads. Trim away fur pile under each eye then glue eyes securely in place and snip off coloured threads.

For mouth work a 2 cm ($\frac{3}{4}$ in) straight stitch down centre seam of face, 3 cm ($1\frac{1}{4}$ in) below point A. Work a curved line in straight stitches below this line. For the nose cut a tiny heart-shape from black felt and glue it in place above the first mouth stitch.

To make ears first trim off 5 mm ($\frac{1}{4}$ in) all round each contrasting lining piece. Join ear pieces to these, easing to fit and leaving lower edges open. Turn ears right side out, fold in half and oversew lower raw edges together. Ladder stitch ears at top of head, where shown by the dotted line on the side head pattern.

Join arm pieces in pairs, leaving a gap at top where shown. Turn and stuff to within 5 cm (2 in) of top. Turn in and slip stitch gap then sew arms to each side of body, about 2 cm ($\frac{3}{4}$ in) down from neck.

Cut tail from fleece or felt and slip stitch it to body where shown on pattern, enclosing a bit of stuffing.

Mrs Bunny's clothes

Notes: 1 cm ($\frac{3}{8}$ in) seams are allowed unless stated otherwise. Draw out the patterns on to metric graph paper as for bunny patterns.

Cut out all clothes as directed on patterns.

Petticoat and pantaloons

You will need: 50 cm ($\frac{5}{8}$ yd) of 91 cm (36 in) wide fabric; 1·60 m ($1\frac{3}{4}$ yd) of lace edging; 70 cm ($\frac{3}{4}$ yd) of narrow elastic; 50 m ($\frac{5}{8}$ yd) of narrow bias binding; two snap fasteners.

To make pantaloons: Hem lower leg edges, taking 1 cm ($\frac{3}{8}$ in) turnings twice, then sew on lace edging. Sew bias binding to the wrong side of each leg piece where shown by dotted lines on pattern. Thread lengths of elastic through each to fit round legs and securely sew elastic at each end.

Join pantaloon pieces at centre, clip seams at curves. Bring centre seams together and join inside leg edges. Hem waist edge, taking 1 cm ($\frac{3}{8}$ in) turnings twice, then thread through elastic to fit waist.

To make petticoat: Cut a fabric strip 20 by 60 cm (8 by $23\frac{1}{2}$ in). Join the short edges, leaving an 8 cm (3 in) gap at top of seam. Turn in and stitch raw edges of gap to neaten. Hem lower edge, taking 1 cm ($\frac{3}{8}$ in) turnings twice, then sew on lace trim.

Gather upper edge to measure 28 cm (11 in) then bind it with 6 by 32 cm ($2\frac{3}{8}$ by $12\frac{1}{2}$ in) straight strip of fabric, leaving 2 cm ($\frac{3}{4}$ in) at one end for an overlap.

Put petticoat on bunny, with top of waistband about 4 cm ($1\frac{1}{2}$ in) down from neck. Pin a strip of lace edging across front of band then up over each shoulder and across back of band to centre back, mitring the corners. Sew in position as pinned, then sew snap fasteners to back of band.

Dress

You will need: 30 cm ($\frac{3}{8}$ yd) of 91 cm (36 in) wide fabric; 1·50 m ($1\frac{5}{8}$ yd) of 4 cm ($1\frac{1}{2}$ in) wide broderie Anglaise or other lace trimming; 1·30 m ($1\frac{1}{2}$ yd) of narrow ribbon; two snap fasteners.

To make: For skirt cut a fabric strip 22 by 91 cm ($8\frac{3}{4}$ by 36 in). Make as for petticoat, trimming lower edge as illustrated. Gather top to measure 29 cm ($11\frac{1}{2}$ in); bind as for petticoat, with a fabric strip 6 by 33 cm ($2\frac{3}{8}$ by 13 in).

For each shoulder strap cut a fabric strip 6 by 15 cm ($2\frac{3}{8}$ by 6 in). Fold, bringing the long edges together, and join all round the raw edges, leaving a gap for turning. Trim seam, turn right side out and slip stitch gap.

Put skirt on bunny and place straps over shoulders, tucking and pinning ends 2 cm ($\frac{3}{4}$ in) inside waistband. Sew straps in place as pinned. Cut the 4 cm ($1\frac{1}{2}$ in) trimming to measure about 3 cm ($1\frac{1}{4}$ in) wide, turn in raw edge then sew trimming to straps and across waistband as illustrated, making tucks at each corner. Sew a ribbon bow to front and snap fasteners to back of band.

Hat

You will need: Small pieces of fabric, interlining and bias binding; 50 cm ($\frac{5}{8}$ yd) of trimming to match dress; oddments of ribbon, flowers, etc., for trimming.

To make: Cut two hat pieces from fabric and one from interlining. Place them together with right sides of fabric facing and the interlining pieces on top of them. Join round edges, taking 5 mm ($\frac{1}{4}$ in) seam and leaving a gap for turning. Turn right side out, slip stitch gap then top stitch round close to edge. Bind earholes to neaten.

Gather the 50 cm ($\frac{5}{8}$ yd) of trimming to fit round dotted line shown on pattern, and sew it in place. Put hat on bunny and take a strip of ribbon under chin, sewing it to positions shown on hat pattern. Trim hat with gathered rosettes of ribbon.

Parasol

Use a 30 cm ($\frac{3}{8}$ yd) strip of thick bootlace for the handle (the type used for sportswear). Push stuffing inside the strip from each end, using a knitting needle, until an 18 cm (7 in) section is stuffed. Trim off excess boot lace, then turn in raw edges and oversew to neaten.

Cut a 19 cm ($7\frac{1}{2}$ in) diameter circle of fabric and sew lace trimming all round raw edge.

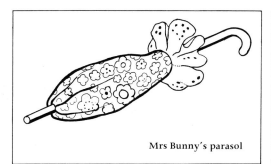

Mrs Bunny's parasol

Snip a small hole at centre of circle and push one end of handle through. Sew fabric to handle at this point and glue a bit of ribbon around. Gather round the circle below lace trim, pull up gathers and sew to handle. Sew a strip of ribbon round gathers.

The parasol can be fixed in place with a piece of Velcro touch-and-close fastener, sewing the other half to bunny's hand.

Mr Bunny's Clothes

Note: 5 mm ($\frac{1}{4}$ in) seams are allowed on all felt pieces. Copy patterns as before.

Trousers

Use striped fabric, and make as for pantaloons, omitting lace trim and leg elastic, etc.

Waistcoat

You will need: Small pieces of felt; buttons.

To make waistcoat: Join fronts to back at shoulders and sides. Top stitch close to edges. Sew buttons to right front edge and make buttonholes in left front.

Coat

You will need: A piece of felt 25 by 50 cm ($9\frac{3}{4}$ by $19\frac{1}{2}$ in).

To make coat: Cut centre back of coat open as far as point A. Top stitch all round coat, 5 mm ($\frac{1}{4}$ in) from edges except for armholes and shoulders. Fold back lapels at dotted line positions and press, then tack top edges to

shoulders. Join front shoulders to back shoulders.

Top stitch 5 mm ($\frac{1}{4}$ in) from wrist edges of sleeves. Join underarm edges of sleeves, turn right side out. Slip armhole edges of sleeves inside armhole edges of coat, matching points B and C. Sew sleeves into armholes, easing tops to fit as on pattern.

Top hat

You will need: A piece of felt 20 by 60 cm (8 by $23\frac{1}{2}$ in); the same amount of interlining; 30 cm ($\frac{3}{8}$ yd) of ribbon for hat band; adhesive.

To make: For a hat brim pattern, draw out a 14 cm ($5\frac{1}{2}$ in) diameter circle with a 9 cm ($3\frac{1}{2}$ in) diameter circle cut out of centre. Cut two brims from felt and one from interlining. Trim 5 mm ($\frac{1}{4}$ in) off outer and inner edges of interlining piece. Glue this centrally between felt brim pieces. Stitch round felt brim, close to outer and inner edges.

For crown of hat cut a felt strip 9 by 29 cm ($3\frac{1}{2}$ by $11\frac{1}{2}$ in), and an interlining strip 8 by 29 cm (3 by $11\frac{1}{2}$ in). Glue interlining centrally to felt. Join short edges.

For top of hat cut a 10 cm (4 in) diameter circle of felt and glue a 9 cm ($3\frac{1}{2}$ in) diameter circle of interlining to the centre. Place this on top of crown piece, with wrong sides outside, then back stitch all round through the 5 mm ($\frac{1}{4}$ in) felt edges. Turn right side out and place on top of hat brim, then oversew the 5 mm ($\frac{1}{4}$ in) felt edges together. Curl up the brim at each side of the hat and glue a ribbon strip round hat.

Cravat

Make a bow shape from a piece of wide ribbon, then use a strip of the same ribbon folded to make a narrower width for the neck band. Sew bow to front of band and a snap fastener to back edges.

Walking stick

Make as for parasol handle, stuffing it to make a 20 cm (8 in) length. Curve the top of the stick by running a thread along then pulling the thread tight and fastening off. Fix to hand as for parasol.

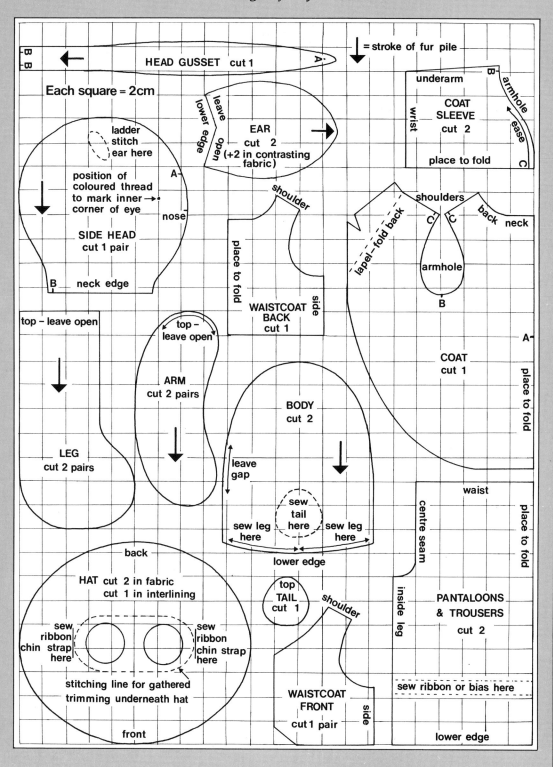

HEAD GUSSET cut 1

B B

A

↓ = stroke of fur pile

Each square = 2cm

underarm

B

COAT
SLEEVE
cut 2

wrist

armhole ease

place to fold

C

ladder
stitch
ear here

leave open

lower edge

EAR
cut 2
(+2 in contrasting
fabric)

→

position of
coloured thread
to mark inner →
corner of eye

A

nose

shoulder

shoulders

lapel-fold back

C C

back neck

SIDE HEAD
cut 1 pair

place to fold

armhole

B neck edge

side

WAISTCOAT
BACK
cut 1

B

A

top – leave open

top –
leave open

COAT
cut 1

place to fold

ARM
cut 2 pairs

BODY
cut 2

LEG
cut 2 pairs

leave
gap

sew
tail
here

sew leg
here

sew leg
here

centre seam

waist

place to fold

lower edge

back

HAT cut 2 in fabric
cut 1 in interlining

top
TAIL
cut 1

shoulder

inside leg

PANTALOONS
& TROUSERS

cut 2

sew
ribbon
chin strap
here

sew
ribbon
chin strap
here

stitching line for gathered
trimming underneath hat

front

WAISTCOAT
FRONT

cut 1 pair

side

sew ribbon or bias here

lower edge

44

Mother and Baby Panda

This lovable pair are both made from soft furry fabric. The eyes and noses are felt and are sewn in place so the toys are safe even for babies to play with. The pandas' legs are sewn in position to enable them to sit steadily. The mother measures about 34 cm (13½ in) and the baby about 21 cm (8¼ in) from top to tail

For the mother and baby panda you will need: 50 cm (½ yd) each of 138 cm (54 in) wide white and black fur fabric (the white is for the heads and bodies and the black is for the arms, legs, ears and eyes); scraps of black and brown felt; white thread; black double knitting yarn; 750 g (1½ lb) of stuffing; adhesive; metric graph paper; black and white button thread for sewing limbs and head in position.

Notes: 1 cm (⅜ in) seams are allowed on all pieces.

Cut pieces from either white or black fur fabric as stated in list of materials, following cutting directions on pattern pieces.

Mark darts, etc. on the wrong side of the fabric.

Copy all the pattern pieces square by square on to graph paper (each square on the diagram equals 5 cm). Mark all the details on to the pattern pieces.

Mother Panda

Sew dart in each side head piece as shown on the pattern then trim the dart. Join side head pieces from point A to neck edge down the centre front. Insert head gusset from point A along top of head to neck edge. Turn head right side out and stuff firmly pushing the stuffing well into 'snout' and above the darts. Run strong gathering thread round neck edge 1 cm (⅜ in) from the edge, pull up gathers turning in the raw edges then oversew to close completely.

Stitch darts on body pieces as shown on the pattern then trim darts. Join body pieces leaving the neck edge open. Turn, stuff and gather neck edge as for head. Place head on top of body matching the gathered portions, centre front seams and taking care to keep back of head and back of body in line with each other. Turn head slightly to one side then push it down on to body and secure with darning needles. Ladder stitch head and body together securely all round twice using strong white thread.

Join each inner arm piece to outer arm piece as far as points A and B. Turn arms right side out and stuff. Slip stitch raw edges at tops of inner arms to the wrong side of outer arms piece to enclose stuffing. Turn in remaining raw edges of outer arms piece 1 cm (⅜ in) and tack. Place this portion around back of panda matching centre fold line to centre back seam of body and having top edge level with line where head joins body. Sew in place using strong black thread then continue ladder stitching tops of arms to body at each side where they touch.

On one pair of leg pieces, make darts as shown on the pattern. Join each of these pieces to the other leg pieces without darts, leaving a gap in the seam for turning as shown on the pattern. Turn and stuff legs then turn in raw edges and slip stitch gaps. Place legs in 'seated' position at each side of the body as illustrated with darted sides of the legs against the body. Secure legs with darning needles then ladder stitch to body where they touch using strong black thread.

Join ears in pairs leaving lower edges open. Turn right side out then oversew lower raw edges together pulling stitches to gather slightly. Sew ears to top of head as shown on head pattern. For mouth, work a shallow W using double black yarn about 2 cm (¾ in) below end of 'snout' as shown in illustration. Cut nose from black felt and stick to end of 'snout'. Cut one pair of eye patch pieces from black fur fabric. Clip fur pile short all over the pieces. Cut eyes from brown felt and pupils from black felt as shown on eye patch pattern.

Stick pupils to eyes then use white thread to work a small highlight on each one as shown in illustration. Stick felt eyes securely to eye patches then pin eyes in position as illustrated. Stick patches in position with a little glue spread under the felt eyes then sew patches in place all round the edges.

Baby Panda

Make baby in the same way as mother using the baby panda patterns and ignoring reference to darts on legs. Work mouth 1·5 cm ($\frac{5}{8}$ in) below end of 'snout' and trim seams on ears before turning right side out.

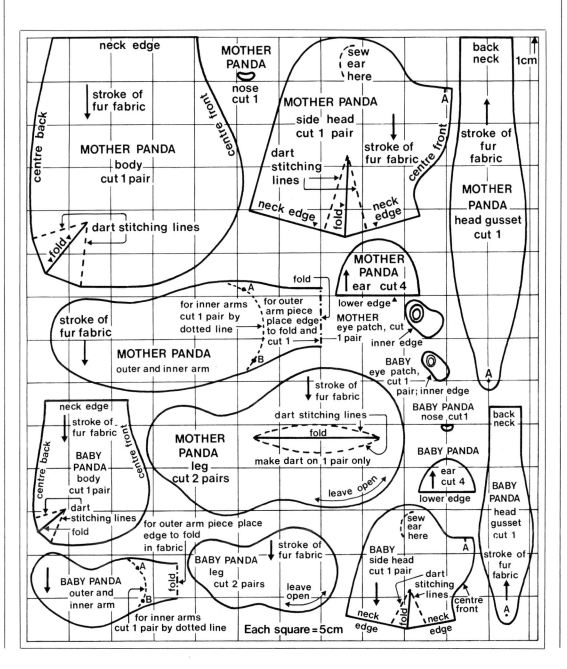

Mother and Baby Bear

A cuddly armful of Teddies comprises Mother Bear, about 38 cm (15 in) tall – she has a dress, apron, bonnet, waist slip and pants – Baby Bear, about 22 cm (8¼ in) complete with dress and pants, and Baby's push-chair, made entirely from fabric

For the bears you will need: 40 cm (16 in) of 138 cm (54 in) wide fur fabric; 250 g (½ lb) of stuffing; scraps of black and brown felt and brown yarn; small piece of Velcro touch and close fastening to match the fur fabric; adhesive.

For Mother Bear's clothes you will need: For the dress: 30 cm (12 in) of 91 cm (36 in) wide fabric; 1·50 m (1⅝ yd) of ric-rac braid; elastic and three snap fasteners.

For the hat and apron: 30 cm (12 in) of 91 cm (36 in) wide fabric; 2 m (2¼ yd) of 2·5 cm (1 in) wide broderie Anglaise edging; elastic; ribbon; one snap fastener.

For panties and underskirt: 30 cm (12 in) of 91 cm (36 in) wide fabric; 1·40 m (1½ yd) of lace edging; elastic; one snap fastener.

For Baby Bear's clothes: Small pieces of fabrics; trimmings; lace; ribbon; elastic; two snap fasteners.

For push-chair you will need: 15 cm (6 in) of 91 cm (36 in) wide quilted fabric; oddments of other fabric; wadding; felt; stuffing; small pieces of Velcro to match the push-chair handle.

Notes: Patterns are given for the bears' heads, ears and bodies, and Baby Bear patterns are printed inside the Mother Bear patterns.

The arms and legs are straight strips of fur fabric and measurements are given in instructions.

Trace body and head gusset patterns on to thin folded paper placing the paper folds at the straight edges of patterns as indicated.

Cut out folded paper and open up to give full-sized patterns.

Have the smooth stroke of fur fabric as shown on patterns and in a downward direction on legs and arms.

The seam allowance is 5 mm (¼ in) seams on all fabric pieces unless otherwise stated. For hems on Mother Bear's clothes take 1 cm (⅜ in) turnings twice, for Baby Bear hems take 5 mm (¼ in) turnings twice.

Mother Bear

Cut one pair of head pieces and one head gusset. Join the head pieces from point A to neck edge. Insert gusset round top of head matching points A and B. Turn and stuff firmly then gather round neck edge with strong thread. Pull up the gathers to close completely then fasten off.

Cut two body pieces and join them leaving a gap in lower edge. Turn and stuff firmly then slip stitch gap. Place gathered portion of head on centre top of body and ladder stitch them together where they touch, working round a few times to secure.

For each leg cut two 8 cm (3 in) by 21 cm (8¼ in) strips of fur fabric. Join them leaving one short end open and rounding off corners at other end. Trim corners, turn right side out and stuff. Turn in remaining raw edges and slip stitch, pulling thread to gather slightly. Sew legs to seam at lower edge of body.

Make arms as for legs using 6 by 15 cm (2⅜ by 6 in) strips of fur fabric. Round off top corners as well as lower corners when sewing, leaving a gap in top. Turn and stuff very loosely. Sew arms to front of body seams 2 cm (¾ in) down from neck.

To make feet, turn up a 6 cm (2⅜ in) portion at end of each leg at right angles to leg. Ladder stitch at fold to hold in place, pulling stitches up tight.

Cut ear pieces and join in pairs leaving lower edges open. Turn right side out then turn in lower edges and oversew, pulling stitches to gather slightly. Sew ears in position

48

at top of head placing them 5 cm (2 in) apart.

Cut eyes from black felt and nose from brown felt. Work a highlight on each eye with small white stitches. Place eyes in position as illustrated. Trim the fur pile shorter below and around snout and also below position of eyes. Stick eyes and nose in place. Spread a small piece of black felt on back with glue and leave to dry. From this cut a 5 mm by 5 cm ($\frac{1}{4}$ by 2 in) strip for mouth. Pin mouth in place as illustrated 2·5 cm (1 in) below nose and sew in position with matching thread.

Cut two small ovals of furry Velcro. Sew one to each hand at position of paw pads so that hands can be fixed to push-chair handle.

Baby Bear

Notes: Make exactly as given for Mother Bear, using Baby Bear patterns plus 3·5 by 9 cm ($1\frac{3}{8}$ by $3\frac{1}{2}$ in) strips of fur fabric for legs and 3 by 7 cm ($1\frac{1}{4}$ by $2\frac{3}{4}$ in) strips for arms.

Make feet as for Mother turning up a 2 cm ($\frac{3}{4}$ in) portion at ends of legs. Do not turn in raw edges when oversewing bases of arms, legs and ears.

Work mouth in brown yarn 1·5 cm ($\frac{5}{8}$ in) below nose.

Mother Bear's clothes

To make the panties: Cut a 12 by 42 cm ($4\frac{3}{4}$ by $16\frac{1}{2}$ in) strip of fabric. Hem both long edges then sew lace trim to one long edge then sew lace trim to one long edge for lower edge of panties. Thread elastic through both hems to fit round bear's waist and top of legs. Join short edges of strip. At the lower edge, catch the seam to the centre front of the panties with a few secure stitches to divide into separate legs.

To make the dress: Cut one pair back bodice pieces. Cut one front placing dotted line in pattern to fold in fabric. Join front to backs at shoulders. Sew ric-rac round neck edge taking care to clear seam allowance. Cut two sleeves placing pattern to fold in fabric. Hem lower edges and thread elastic through to fit bear's arms. Run gathering threads along armhole edges of sleeves between dots. Join armholes of sleeves to bodice armholes pulling up sleeves into gathers to fit. Join entire underarm edges of sleeves and sides of bodice. Hem centre back edges of bodice then bind neck edge with 2·5 cm (1 in) wide bias strip of fabric.

For dress skirt, cut a 16 by 91 cm ($6\frac{1}{4}$ by 36 in) strip of fabric. Hem one long edge and sew on ric-rac. Join short edges from hem edge for 7 cm ($2\frac{3}{4}$ in), taking a 1 cm ($\frac{3}{8}$ in) seam. Neaten remainder of these edges and press seam to one side. Gather top of skirt to fit lower edge of bodice then sew in place. Sew snap fasteners to back of bodice.

To make the underskirt: Make as for dress skirt sewing lace to hem and gathering waist edge to fit round bear. Bind the gathered edge with a 4 by 34 cm ($1\frac{1}{2}$ by $13\frac{1}{2}$ in) strip of fabric for the waistband. Sew snap fastener to back of band.

To make the cap: Cut two 30 cm (12 in) diameter circles of fabric. Gather the length of broderie Anglaise trimming slightly all along the raw edge. Sew the gathered edge of trimming all round edge of one circle having raw edges level. Cut off excess trimming and set aside for apron. Now join cap circles round edges leaving a gap in seam. Turn right side out and press but do not slip stitch gap. To form casing for elastic, stitch round cap 3 cm ($1\frac{1}{4}$ in) from seam, then stitch round again 2 cm ($\frac{3}{4}$ in) from the seam, leaving a gap in this line of stitching opposite gap in cap seam. Cut a length of elastic to fit bear's head and thread it through casing passing it through gap in seam. Join ends of elastic and stitch gaps. Sew ribbon bow to front of cap.

To make the apron: Cut two 10 by 14 cm (4 by $5\frac{1}{2}$ in) pieces of fabric. Round off two corners at one long edge for lower corners of apron. Sew trimming round edge of apron except for the straight long edge, with raw edges level. Join apron pieces leaving straight long edges open. Turn, then gather raw edges to measure 10 cm (4 in). For waistband cut a 4 by 36 cm ($1\frac{1}{2}$ by 14 in) strip of fabric. Bind top of apron with centre portion of this strip then turn in raw edges folding band in half. Stitch all round band. Sew snap fastener to ends of band.

Put apron on bear and pin two strips of gathered trimming to inside of waistband at back and front taking one over each shoulder. Remove these shoulder straps and bind raw edges of trimming with 3 cm ($1\frac{1}{4}$ in) wide strips of fabric. Sew straps to waistband as pinned previously.

Baby's Bear's clothes

To make the panties: Make as for Mother's using a 7 by 25 cm ($2\frac{3}{4}$ by $9\frac{3}{4}$ in) strip of fabric.

To make the dress: Make as for Mother's using Baby Bear bodice patterns plus a 7 by 40 cm ($2\frac{3}{4}$ by 16 in) strip of fabric for the skirt. Join back edges of skirt for 2 cm ($\frac{3}{4}$ in) only and bind neck edge with a 2 cm ($\frac{3}{4}$ in) wide bias strip. Sew ribbon bow to neck edge at front. Sew ribbon bow to Baby Bear's head.

Push-chair

When sewing the quilted push-chair pieces together, place them right sides together and position the wadding piece on top.

For the seat cut two 11 cm ($4\frac{1}{4}$ in) squares of quilted fabric and one of wadding. Join round edges leaving a gap for turning. Turn right side out and slip stitch gap. Machine stitch all round 1 cm ($\frac{3}{8}$ in) from edges. For strip which goes round sides and back of chair cut two 7 by 32 cm ($2\frac{3}{4}$ by $12\frac{1}{2}$ in) pieces of quilted fabric and one of wadding. Round off corners at one long edge on all pieces then make as for seat. Pin long edge of this strip round three sides of seat; then on outside, pin a small tuck from corners of seat upwards. Stitch tucks as pinned. Oversew strip to seat as pinned previously.

Make back support as for seat rounding off corners at one edge. Place in position at back of chair and sew in place.

For footrest cut two 7 by 11 cm ($2\frac{3}{4}$ by $4\frac{1}{4}$ in) pieces of quilted fabric and one of wadding. Make as for other pieces. Fold piece, bringing long edges together, then machine stitch across fold. Oversew one long edge of footrest to front edge of seat.

For each wheel cut a 15 cm (6 in) diameter circle of fabric. Mark centre of circle on outside of fabric. Gather edges of circles and stuff, then pull up gathers to close and fasten off. Stab stitch through wheels to marked centre of circle a few times, pulling stitches tight. Cut four 2 cm ($\frac{3}{4}$ in) diameter circles of felt and sew one to gathered centre of each wheel. Pin wheels to push-chair as illustrated then sew them in place where they touch.

For handle of push-chair cut a 6 by 50 cm ($2\frac{3}{8}$ by $19\frac{1}{2}$ in) strip of fabric. Join long edges and across one short end. Turn right side out by pushing sewn end through with a knitting needle. Trim off the sewn end and then stuff the handle from each end with a knitting needle. Turn in raw edges and slip stitch. Pin handle to back of push-chair at each side as illustrated having ends level with seat of chair. Sew handle in place where it touches push-chair. Bend handle back slightly and stitch folds level with top of back rest to hold in place. Stitch a fold at top of handle at each side to form squared off shape. Sew a strip of hooked Velcro to handle top at each side (so the handle can be attached to Mother Bear's paws).

For safety bar cut a 3 by 10 cm ($1\frac{1}{4}$ by 4 in) strip of fabric. Make as for handle then sew ends in place as illustrated.

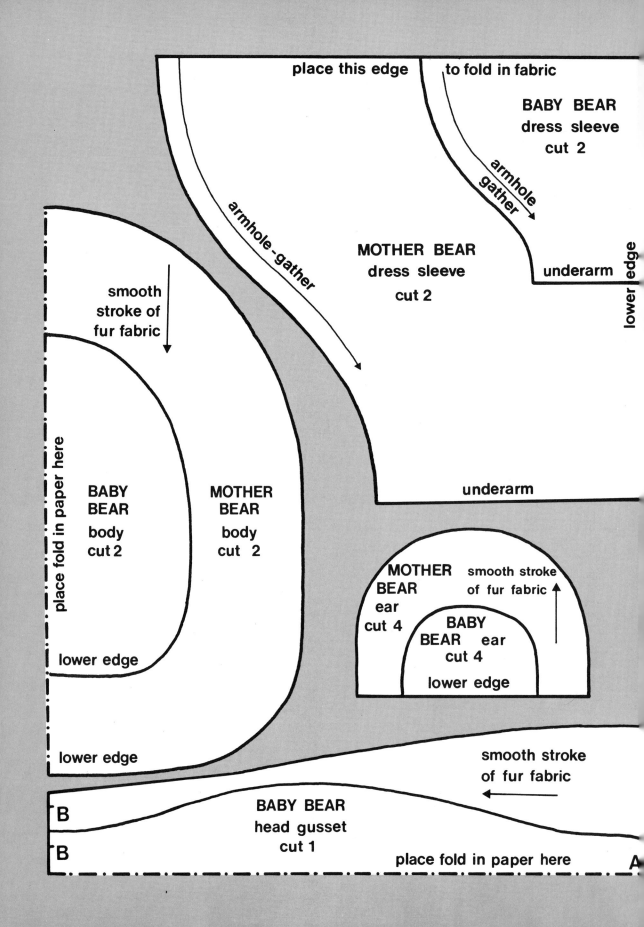

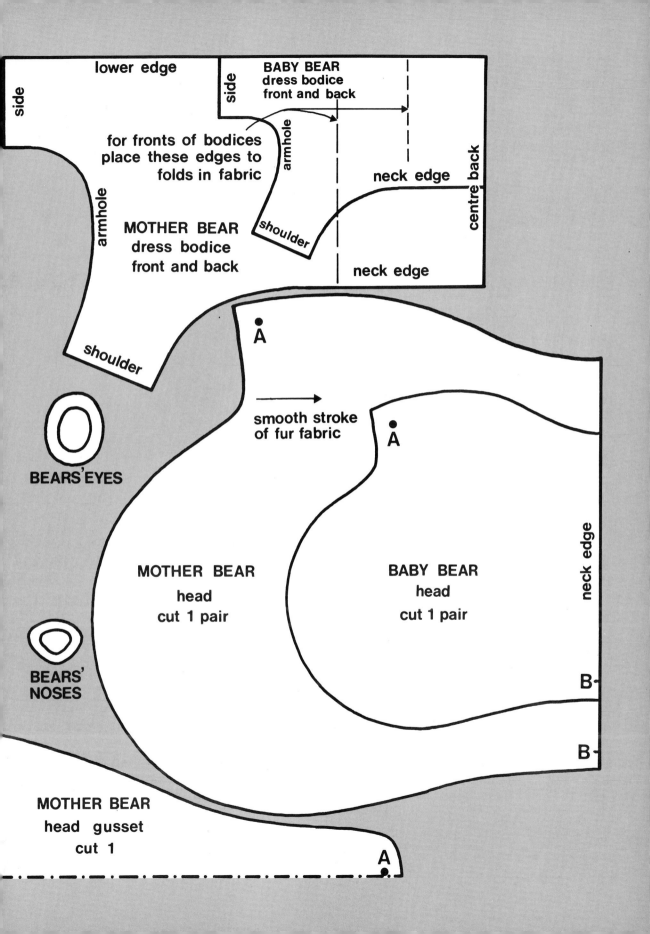

2
SIT-UPON
TOYS

Leo the Laughing Lion · 56
Ladybird, Ladybird · 59

Leo the Laughing Lion

Leo the friendly Lion is more than just a toy to sit on and hug; at 84 cm (33 in) long and 40 cm (16 in) high from paw to mane, he will guard your door so well that no draught will ever dare to enter!

You will need: 1·20 m ($1\frac{1}{8}$ yd) of 138 cm (54 in) wide short pile fur fabric; 40 cm ($\frac{1}{2}$ yd) of 138 cm (54 in) wide long hair fur fabric (see suppliers' list on page 139); 1·5 kilo (3 lb) of stuffing; scraps of black, blue and white felt; thick black football laces for mouth and pawlines; metric graph paper.

For the patterns: Copy the outlines from scaled-down diagram on to metric graph paper, noting that each square on diagram equals 5 cm.

Cut out all the patterns, then cut a second body pattern, making the outline exactly the same as the first. On one body pattern cut out the circular shape shown by the broken line on pattern (this is the *upper body* pattern). Mark points C and D on this piece also.

On the other body pattern mark the dart lines as shown on pattern – this is the *underbody* pattern. Mark all lettering on each pattern piece.

Notes: All pieces are cut from short-pile fur fabric except for the mane and tail end (cut these from long-hair fabric).

Pin patterns to wrong side of fabric as shown on the cutting-out layout.

Mark all points, A, B, C, etc., shown on the pattern pieces on the wrong side of fur fabric pieces.

The seam allowance is 1 cm ($\frac{3}{8}$ in) on all pieces unless otherwise stated. Join all pieces with right sides facing.

Leo the Lion

Start with the head. Join centre front edges of face pieces as far as points A. Sew sides of face gusset to top edges of face pieces, matching points A and B. Join centre front and centre back edges of back head pieces,

leaving a gap in centre back seam as shown on pattern. Now join back head and face pieces to each other at the side face edges, matching the centre front seams.

Sew the lower edges of head to the cut-out circular shape in the upper body, matching points C and D on both pieces. On the underbody piece stitch the dart as marked. Now join both body pieces all round edges, leaving the back leg edges open. Clip the seam at front between legs.

Join the inner and outer back leg pieces round the foot from points E to F, leaving the top edges open. Now join the back legs to the body as follows. First sew top edges of the outer leg pieces to the leg edges of the upper body, easing the leg edges to fit the body and matching points E and F. Now sew the top edges of the inner leg piece to the leg edges of the underbody.

Turn the lion right side out through the gap in head seam. Stuff the lion firmly, beginning with the front legs, then the back legs followed by the body and head. Ladder stitch the opening in the seam.

Join the side edges of the tail, leaving top edges open. Turn right side out and stuff lightly. Join the tail end pieces together, turn right side out and stuff as for tail pieces. Slip narrow end of tail inside top edges of tail end piece, then turn in raw edges and sew them to tail. Turn in and sew top of tail very securely to back of body below centre back seam.

Join centre front and centre back edges of mane pieces. With mane wrong side out, place face edge over lion's face, making sure the raw edge is level with lion's side face seam. Also place centre front of mane at centre front of lion's face under chin. Back stitch mane to head 3 cm ($1\frac{1}{4}$ in) away from raw edge at top of head, tapering to 1 cm ($\frac{3}{8}$ in) away from raw edge beneath chin. Pull mane back over lion's head, turning it right side out. Slip stitch lower raw edge of mane to back and sides of lion's body where they touch.

Join ear pieces in pairs, leaving lower edges open. Turn right side out then turn in lower edges. Oversew lower edges together, pulling stitches tightly to gather slightly. Brush long pile on mane forward at top of head, then sew ears to face just in front of mane seam and each side of face gusset.

For mouth lines cut two 13 cm (5⅛ in) lengths of bootlace. Back stitch centre of strips to face as shown by broken line on face pattern. Clip fur pile slightly shorter above

mouth lines up to position of nose. Cut nose from black felt and sew it to face, with lower end just overlapping top of mouth lines.

Cut all eye pieces as directed on the pattern and sew them together. Work a highlight on each pupil in white thread. Sew eyes to face each side of face gusset, 5 cm (2 in) up from nose.

For lines on each paw, cut three 8 cm (3 in) long strips of bootlace. Back stitch them in place as shown in illustration.

Cutting-out layout for short pile fur fabric pieces

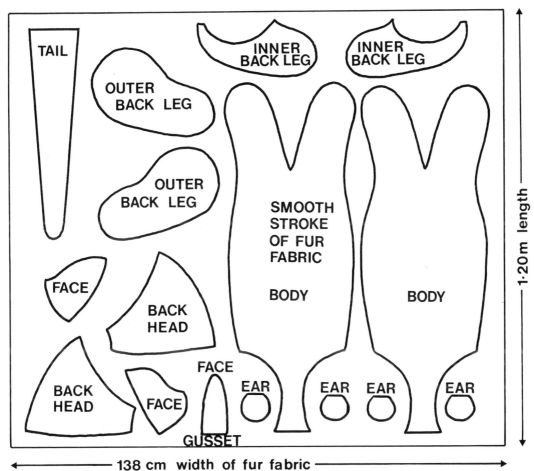

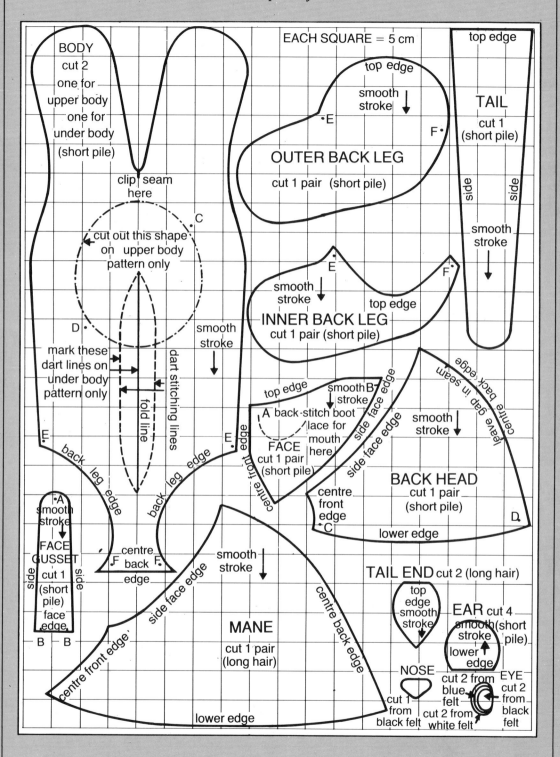

Ladybird, Ladybird

Mother ladybird – a giant-sized pouffe for the nursery – measures 46 cm (18 in) long, while her baby, only about 23 cm (9 in) from head to tail, makes an appealing small soft toy

For both ladybirds you will need: 40 by 138 cm (16 by 54 in) of red fur fabric; 50 by 138 cm (20 by 54 in) of black fabric; 1·5 kg (3 lb) stuffing; felt and thread for facial features; 1 m (1⅛ yd) of frilled lace edging and 1·50 m (1⅝ yd) of broad ribbon for large ladybird; small pieces of lace trimming and narrow ribbon for small ladybird; metric graph paper.

Notes: The seam allowance is 1 cm (⅜ in) on all pieces unless stated otherwise. Join the fabrics with right sides facing.

Copy all the pattern pieces square by square, on to graph paper (each square on diagram equals 2 cm). Mark all details on patterns.

Ladybird pouffe

Cut out a pair of large upper body pieces from red fur fabric; and a pair of large face pieces and one large underbody from black fabric (note that underbody pattern should be placed to a fold in fabric where directed on pattern). Mark points A, B, C and D, and positions of legs, on wrong side of fabric pieces.

Join each face piece to an upper body piece, matching points A-B. Now join the entire body and face pieces along top seam, from points C to C, leaving a gap in seam where shown on upper body pattern.

Cut six pairs of large leg pieces from black fabric. Join them in pairs leaving the straight edges open. Trim seams, turn right side out and stuff legs lightly, then sew straight edges of each leg together.

Place legs on underbody piece at positions shown on pattern, with legs pointing towards centre of underbody and raw edges of legs and underbody level.

Join the upper body to underbody, matching points C and D and easing upper body to fit underbody all round. Turn right side out and stuff very firmly, then ladder stitch the opening.

For the spots cut seven 9 cm (3½ in) diameter circles of black fabric. Turn in the raw edges 5 mm (¼ in) and tack. Pin one spot on top of the ladybird, and three on each side

(as shown in illustration). Slip stitch the spots in place.

Cut eyes, pupils and nose from felts, using the patterns (see illustration as a guide to colours). Sew the pupils to the eyes and work a few white stitches on each pupil for a highlight. For cheeks cut two 7 cm (2¾ in) diameter circles of felt.

For mouth draw a U-shaped line on face, 7 cm (2¾ in) up from seam at the front. Work mouth in red thread, then position and sew on felt features, using illustration as a guide.

Sew two rows of lace frilling round the face, then sew ends of ribbon lengths to each side of frilling to tie in a bow below the mouth. Sew the bow in place. Make two ribbon rosettes and sew one to each side of the ribbon.

The baby ladybird

Make this in exactly the same way as for the large ladybird, using the small pattern pieces. For the spots cut 6 cm (2⅜ in) diameter circles of fabric, and 5 cm (2 in) diameter circles of felt for the cheeks. Work the mouth 3 cm (1¼ in) up from seam.

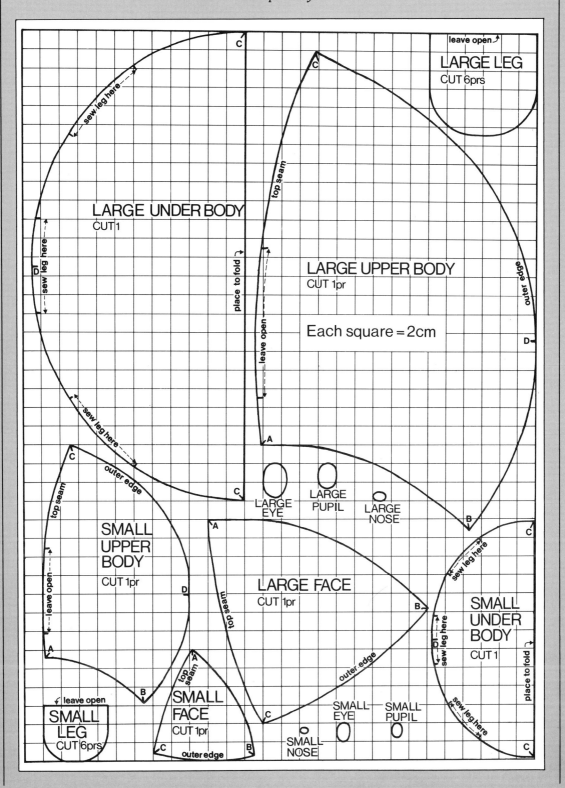

LARGE LEG
CUT 6prs
leave open

sew leg here

LARGE UNDER BODY
CUT 1

top seam

sew leg here

place to fold

LARGE UPPER BODY
CUT 1pr

leave open

outer edge

Each square = 2cm

D

A

sew leg here

C

C

LARGE EYE

LARGE PUPIL

LARGE NOSE

B

C

C

outer edge

A

sew leg here

SMALL UPPER BODY
CUT 1pr

top seam

leave open

top seam

LARGE FACE
CUT 1pr

B

SMALL UNDER BODY
CUT 1

sew leg here

D

A

B

top seam

D

outer edge

place to fold

leave open

SMALL LEG
CUT 6prs

top seam

A

SMALL FACE
CUT 1pr

C

B

outer edge

C

SMALL NOSE

SMALL EYE

SMALL PUPIL

C

61

3
SMALL
SOFT TOYS

Twelve Simple Toys · 64

The bee · 64
The ladybird · 64
The tortoise · 64
The octopus · 64
The hedgehog · 65
The owl · 65
The koala · 65
The mouse · 65
The rabbit · 66
The dog · 66
The lion · 66
The penguin · 66

Moo and Chew · 67

Twelve Simple Toys

A toymaker's dozen of furry creatures, all designed without having to use a single pattern. The toys are made from simple shapes – squares, circles and oblongs – using fur fabric and felt. Finished sizes range from around 23 cm (9 in) high for the koala, owl and penguin, and 23 cm (9 in) long for the puppy and lion, down to 10 cm (4 in) nose to tail for the busy bee and the ladybird

For all the animals you will need: Oddments of fur fabric; stuffing; scraps of felt, fleecy fabric, trimmings and ribbon; adhesive; strong thread for gathering fur fabric.

Notes: All the animals are made from fur fabric with felt for features. 1 cm ($\frac{3}{8}$ in) seams are allowed unless otherwise stated.

Some animals are made from fur fabric circles. For this run a strong gathering thread round close to circle edges, pull up gathers slightly, insert stuffing then gather tightly and fasten off. Cover gap by sewing on a 5 cm (2 in) diameter felt circle.

Have the smooth stroke of fur fabric going from front to back or from top to bottom of the toys. Snip away fur pile under facial features before glueing in place.

On rectangular pieces with rounded-off corners, trim off excess fabric at these corners before turning right side out.

The bee

Gather and stuff an 18 cm (7 in) diameter circle of yellow fur fabric. For stripes cut three 2 cm ($\frac{3}{4}$ in) wide strips of black fur fabric; place strips round body, catch ends together beneath body, sew them in place.

For eyes glue 5 mm ($\frac{1}{4}$ in) diameter felt circles on larger ovals. Use a smaller fur fabric circle for nose. Make loops of black thread above eyes as illustrated.

For each wing cut a 12 cm ($4\frac{3}{4}$ in) diameter circle of net. Fold in half and gather folded edge, sew wings to bee.

The ladybird

Make as for bee, gathering a 16 cm ($6\frac{1}{4}$ in) diameter red fur fabric circle. Sew on black ric-rac trimming and ten 1 cm ($\frac{3}{8}$ in) diameter black felt circles for spots.

The tortoise

Gather and stuff a 30 cm (12 in) diameter circle of fur fabric. Sew on flower trimming for shell markings, as illustrated.

For head cut two 9 by 11 cm ($3\frac{1}{2}$ by $4\frac{1}{4}$ in) strips of contrasting fleece. Join round edges, rounding off corners at one short edge and leaving other short edges open. Turn, stuff, gather raw edges and sew to tortoise close to base. Catch head to body a little further up to hold it upright. Make eyes and nose as for bee.

For each foot cut two 6 cm ($2\frac{3}{8}$ in) squares of fleece. Join as for head, turn and stuff, then oversew raw edges to body as illustrated. Sew frilled trimming in place to complete.

The octopus

Gather and stuff a 30 cm (12 in) diameter circle of fur fabric. Cut eight fur fabric strips 8 by 24 cm (3 by $9\frac{1}{2}$ in), join long edges of each and across one short edge, rounding off corners. Turn right side out. Sew raw ends to octopus – round edge of felt circle. For eyes glue 2 cm ($\frac{3}{4}$ in) diameter felt circles on larger ovals, as illustrated.

The hedgehog

Cut two 22 cm (8¾ in) radius quarter-circles of fur fabric. Mark both at centre point of circle, noting that this is the back of the hedgehog, close to base. Round off one of the remaining corners using a big curve for humped back of hedgehog. Round off remaining corner slightly for snout. Join pieces leaving a gap in base. Turn and stuff, then slip stitch gap.

To turn up the snout run a strong gathering thread from snout 8 cm (3 in) up back seam, pull up gathers and fasten off.

For face piece cut a 14 cm (5½ in) diameter semi-circle of felt. Fold it into a quarter-circle and round off point. Oversew along straight edges and round point. Turn, put a little stuffing in point, slip this over snout and catch to head.

For each foot cut two 6 cm (2⅜ in) squares of felt. Make as for tortoise.

For nose gather and stuff a 3 cm (1¼ in) diameter felt circle and sew in place. For eyelids cut 1·5 cm (⅝ in) felt squares, rounding off top corners. For eyelashes cut 1 cm (⅜ in) wide felt strips and snip along one edge, glue to eyelids as illustrated.

The owl

Cut two fur fabric pieces 18 by 26 cm (7 by 10¼ in). Join them round edges taking large curves on corners at one short edge and smaller curves at other short edge, and leaving a gap for turning. Turn and stuff, then slip stitch gap. The large curves are the top of the head. Tie strong thread round 13 cm (5 in) down from upper edge.

For each ear cut two fur fabric triangles measuring 10 cm (4 in) across the base by 6 cm (2⅜ in) high. Join in pairs, leaving bases open. Turn, oversew bases to head as illustrated.

For each wing cut a triangle of fur fabric and one of felt measuring 12 cm (4¾ in) across the base by 12 cm (4¾ in) high. Join, rounding off top point and leaving bases open. Turn and oversew raw edges, pulling stitches to gather slightly. Sew to owl.

For each foot cut two 9 cm (3½ in) diameter semi-circles of felt. Join round curves, turn, push in a little stuffing and oversew remaining edges under owl at front, gathering slightly.

For eyes cut felt circles 2, 3 and 4 cm (¾, 1¼ and 1½ in) in diameter. For nose cut a felt triangle 2·5 cm (1 in) across base by 2 cm (¾ in) high; round off corners of triangle. Sew features in place.

The koala

Make body as for owl. Sew an 8 by 12 cm (3 by 4¾ in) piece of white fleece to the front, rounding off the corners. Make ears as for owl, using 7 by 10 cm (2¾ by 4 in) fur fabric rectangles and rounding off corners at one long edge.

For each arm cut two 7 by 8 cm (2¾ by 3 in) fur fabric pieces. Join, rounding off corners at one short edge, leaving opposite edge open. Turn and stuff, then sew to koala as illustrated. For nose cut a fur fabric triangle 4 cm (1½ in) across the base by 4 cm (1½ in) high. Round off corners then sew nose to face, pushing a little stuffing underneath. For eyes use felt circles 1·5 and 2 cm (⅝ and ¾ in) in diameter.

The mouse

Cut a 20 cm (8 in) radius quarter-circle of fur fabric. Fold it, bringing straight edges together, and round off centre point. Oversew round point and along straight edges, pulling up stitches until seam measures about 14 cm (5½ in). Turn, gather round remaining raw edge, stuff and fasten off.

For tail cut a triangle 2·5 cm (1 in) across the base by 15 cm (6 in) high. Round off top point and oversew long edges together then sew tail to back of mouse.

For ears cut two 2·5 by 4 cm (1 by 1½ in) felt pieces, rounding off corners at one long edge. Sew to head gathering ears at base. Make eyes and nose as for bee. Use white threads for whiskers, stiffening them with glue after sewing in place.

The rabbit

Make as for mouse, using a 28 cm (11 in) radius quarter-circle of fur fabric, snipping 7 cm (2¾ in) off centre point and pulling up oversewn seam to measure 18 cm (7 in). Tie strong thread round, 8 cm (3 in) from upper edge.

For each foot cut two 5 by 6 cm (2 by 2⅜ in) pieces of fur fabric. Make as for koala, rounding off corners at one long edge, then sew in place as illustrated. Gather and stuff a 5 cm (2 in) diameter fur fabric circle for tail.

For each ear cut an 8 by 10 cm (3 by 4 in) piece of fur fabric and of fleece. Join them, rounding off corners at one short edge and leaving opposite edges open. Turn and sew to head as illustrated, gathering raw edges. For eyes glue 1·5 cm (⅝ in) diameter felt circles to larger ovals. For nose use a 1·5 cm (⅝ in) diameter circle of felt.

The dog

For body cut two fur fabric pieces 15 by 18 cm (6 by 7 in). Join them, rounding off two corners at one short edge and leaving opposite edges open. Turn, stuff and oversew raw edges, pulling stitches tight to gather slightly.

For each foot cut two 8 cm (3 in) squares of fur fabric. Make as for body. Sew two to front of dog and two to seam at sides for back legs. Bring back legs to standing position and catch them to body to hold them in place.

For head cut two 12 by 14 cm (4¾ by 5½ in) pieces of fur fabric. Join, taking large curves on corners of one short edge, and smaller curves on opposite edge, leaving a gap for turning. Turn and stuff then slip stitch gap. Sew head on body as illustrated, with the small curves at top of head.

For each ear cut an 8 by 13 cm (3 by 5 in) piece of fur fabric and of felt. Make as for rabbit ears and sew to head as illustrated.

For tail cut a triangle measuring 10 cm (4 in) across the base by 8 cm (3 in) high. Join side edges, turn and stuff then sew in place. For eyes glue 1·5 cm (⅝ in) diameter circles of felt over slightly larger ovals; for nose use a 1·5 cm (⅝ in) diameter felt circle.

The lion

Make as for dog, except for head. For this join two 14 cm (5½ in) diameter circles of fur fabric, leaving a gap. Turn, stuff and slip stitch gap then sew to body as for dog.

For mane cut a 4 by 36 cm (1½ by 14 in) strip of shaggy fur fabric and join short edges. Place mane round face, with right sides together and long raw edge about 2 cm (¾ in) away from seam on head. Sew long edge in place then turn mane back over head.

For tail cut a 4 by 16 cm (1½ by 6¼ in) strip of fur fabric. Join long edges and across one short end then turn right side out. Sew a bit of shaggy fur fabric to end of tail.

For eyes use 1·5 and 2 cm (⅝ and ¾ in) diameter felt circles. For nose cut a felt triangle 2 cm (¾ in) across the base, 2 cm (¾ in) high and round off the corners slightly.

The penguin

Cut two pieces of black fur fabric 16 by 24 cm (6¼ by 9½ in). Round off two corners at one short edge for top of head, taking large curves, and round off one remaining corner for front of penguin. Leave the remaining corner square to form the penguin's tail. Join pieces leaving a gap, turn and stuff. Slip stitch gap. Tie thread round, 10 cm (4 in) down from top. Cut a piece of white fleece 9 by 12 cm (3½ by 4¾ in). Round off corners and sew to front as illustrated.

For each foot cut two 7 cm (2¾ in) squares of felt; make and sew them in place as for the rabbit.

For beak cut a triangle measuring 8 cm (3 in) across the base by 7 cm (2¾ in) high. Round off top point then join sides and round point. Turn, stuff, then sew to face as illustrated. Make eyes as for lion.

For each wing cut a fur fabric and a felt triangle measuring 9 cm (3½ in) across the base by 17 cm (6¼ in) high. Snip 7 cm (2¾ in) off top points then round off. Join and sew in place as for owl's wings.

Moo and Chew

These two irresistible miniature cows are about 9 cm (3½ in) long and are just the size to nestle in a toddler's hand, or fit into a pocket

You will need: Small pieces of white fleecy fabric; black and brown permanent marker pens; scraps of pink, black, brown and white felt; strands of brown and green embroidery thread and white yarn; stuffing; small bells and narrow ribbon; adhesive.

Note: The outline on the cow patterns is the stitching line.

The chewing cow

Trace the body and head patterns off the page on to folded pieces of paper, placing folds in paper to dotted lines shown on patterns. Cut out folded patterns and open up to give full-sized patterns.

Pin body pattern on to double layer of fleece, right sides together. Now machine stitch all round close to edge of pattern leaving a gap in seam at front end. Remove pattern and cut out body close to stitching line. Turn body right side out and stuff, then slip stitch gap. Run a gathering thread along centre of one body piece from back to front of body. Pull up thread slightly and fasten off. Fold body along this line bringing legs close together. Ladder stitch along fabric at fold to hold legs in this position.

Make head, turn and stuff as for body leaving gap in seam at top. Slip stitch gap. To make the patched markings on body and head, work irregular areas with brown marker pen as illustrated dabbing with a paper tissue to press colour into fabric. Work over again if necessary to penetrate fleece and deepen colour.

Cut ears from brown felt to match markings. Fold in half at lower edges, oversew these edges then sew to position on head as illustrated. Cut two horns pieces from white felt and oversew them together all round edges leaving a gap at lower edge. Horns may now be turned right sides out and then stuffed. Oversew gap. Cut a 1 by 2 cm ($\frac{3}{8}$ by $\frac{3}{4}$ in) strip of brown felt and wrap length of strip around centre of horns, oversewing short edges together at lower edge. Sew centre of horns in place behind ears.

Cut nose from pink felt and mark on dots for nostrils with black pen. Cut eyes from white felt and smaller ovals from black felt. Glue eye pieces together as shown on head pattern then stick eyes and nose to head.

Use a length of brown thread to work a 1 cm ($\frac{3}{8}$ in) stitch for mouth along seam line at front. For the 'grass' take green threads through from back of head to centre of mouth line and trim to irregular lengths. If available, sew a small guipure flower to one strand of

grass. Now position head on body as illustrated and sew them together.

For tail cut a 1 by 4 cm ($\frac{3}{8}$ by 1$\frac{1}{2}$ in) strip of brown felt. Taper strip slightly towards one end. Oversew long edges together and across short tapered end enclosing a few strands of white yarn. Tease out yarn strands and trim to about 2 cm ($\frac{3}{4}$ in). Put a touch of glue on ends of strands and twist together to form the shape illustrated. Sew tail to back of cow. Thread bell on to ribbon and tie in a bow round cow's neck.

The mooing cow

Make as for chewing cow using black pen for for the markings with white felt for the ears and black for the tail. Sew head in position illustrated. Using white thread take a stitch through head seam at position of mouth, from one corner of mouth to the other. Pull thread tightly and fasten off. Cut a small black felt oval for mouth and stick in place as illustrated. Cut eye ovals from pink felt. Trim a little off across lower edges and stick small strips of black felt to these edges. Snip black felt into eyelashes.

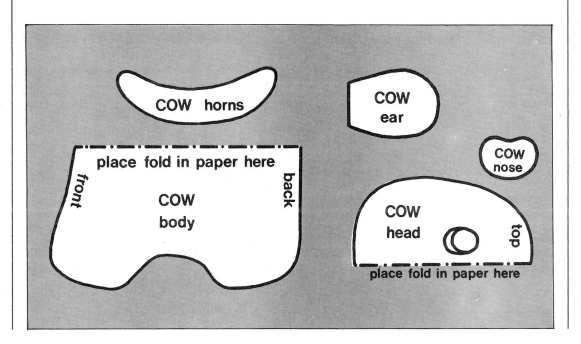

69

4
RAG
DOLLS

Twin Rag Dolls · 72

*The Adaptable Rag Doll
79*

The Well-dressed Doll · 84

Glad-rag Doll · 90

Twin Rag Dolls

Meet the Tearaway Twins, the 48-cm (19-in) high rag dolls – just the right size to play with and cuddle. They have flexible arms and legs and soft short hair that can be brushed this way and that. In addition there is a full set of removable clothes for each doll

For both dolls you need: 50 cm ($\frac{5}{8}$ yd) of 91 cm (36 in) wide pink cotton fabric; 20 cm ($\frac{1}{4}$ yd) of 91 cm (36 in) wide striped or plain fabric for legs; scraps of plain dark fabric for feet; 18 by 44 cm (7 by 17$\frac{1}{2}$ in) strip of fur fabric for hair; 500 g (1 lb) of stuffing; scraps of felt and red and black thread for facial features; red pencil for cheeks; adhesive.

Note about doll pattern on page 78
The body and head is a one-piece pattern but since it is too long to fit on the page, it is printed in two pieces. Trace the body and the head patterns onto thin folded paper, placing folded edge of paper to the dotted lines on patterns when tracing. Mark on all details then cut out patterns with paper still folded. Now open up the patterns and join the head to the body at the neckline with sticky tape, to form the complete one piece pattern. Trace all other patterns off the pages and cut out.

Notes: The seam allowance is 5 mm ($\frac{1}{4}$ in) on all pieces unless otherwise stated. Join fabrics with right sides facing. Cut out all pieces with straight grain of fabric in the direction shown on patterns (the body pieces are cut on bias of fabric).

The dolls

Legs: For each leg cut a fabric strip 14 by 19 cm (5$\frac{1}{2}$ by 7$\frac{1}{2}$ in). From pattern cut two pairs of foot pieces. Join them in pairs at centre front for about 3 cm (1$\frac{1}{4}$ in). Press seam open then join top edge of each foot to one short edge of each leg strip. Press seam down

towards foot then join long edges of leg and remainder of seam round foot pieces. Turn right side out.

Stuff legs firmly to within 3 cm (1$\frac{1}{4}$ in) of top edges. Put a pin through each leg to hold stuffing in place, bringing top edges together so leg seam is at centre back of leg.

Body: Cut two body pieces, making sure they are on the bias of fabric shown on the pattern.

Mark dart lines at neck on wrong side of each fabric piece, then mark positions of facial features lightly on right side of one piece. Fold each piece on neckline then stitch darts along dotted lines. Trim a little off folded edges of darts. Cut two 1 by 7 cm ($\frac{3}{8}$ by 2$\frac{3}{4}$ in) straight strips of pink fabric. Place one beneath each neck dart and stitch again along dart stitching line (this straight strip prevents neck stretching as the body is stuffed).

Join body pieces, leaving top and lower edges open. Turn right side out, turn in lower edges of body 1 cm ($\frac{3}{8}$ in) and tack. Tack top raw edges of each leg together, making a tiny inverted pleat at each side of leg so leg will fit in position shown on lower edge of body pattern. Slip top edges of legs 1 cm ($\frac{3}{8}$ in) between tacked lower edges of body then stitch through body and legs as tacked.

Stuff the body and head firmly. Turn in top raw edges of head and run a strong gathering thread round. Pull up gathers as tightly as possible and fasten off, oversew securely to close any gap. Tie doubled thread tightly round neck at dart lines and sew thread ends into neck.

Arms: Cut two pairs of arm pieces. Join them in pairs round edges leaving upper edges open. Trim seam round hand. Turn and stuff to within 3 cm (1$\frac{1}{4}$ in) of top edges. Take a few stitches through arm at seams 2 cm ($\frac{3}{4}$ in)

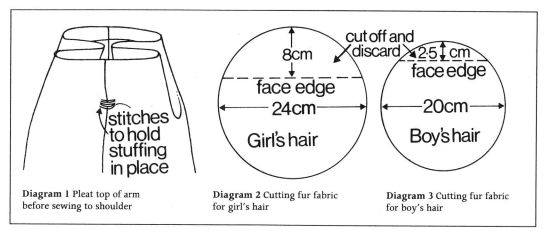

Diagram 1 Pleat top of arm before sewing to shoulder

Diagram 2 Cutting fur fabric for girl's hair

Diagram 3 Cutting fur fabric for boy's hair

down from top edge to hold stuffing in place (see diagram 1). Turn in top raw edges 1 cm ($\frac{3}{8}$ in) and bring seams together making an inverted pleat at each side (see diagram 1). Oversew top edges of each arm together as pleated then sew arms securely to shoulders where shown on pattern.

Face: Mark mouth and nose lines lightly with red pencil then work over mouth with small straight stitches in red. To colour cheeks rub pencil gently over fabric. Work eyelashes with black straight stitches. Cut 1 cm ($\frac{3}{8}$ in) diameter circles of black felt, glue them in place for eyes.

Hair: To make a pattern for girl's hair draw a 24 cm ($9\frac{1}{2}$ in) diameter circle, cut an 8 cm (3 in) section off circle (see diagram 2) and discard it. Using remaining pattern piece, pin pattern on wrong side of fur fabric and cut out carefully snipping through backing to avoid cutting fabric pile.

Gather round edge of fur fabric, pull up gathers, place on head with straight edge around face then pull up gathers to fit head and fasten off. Adjust position of hair on head and sew to head securely all round. Sew a small ribbon bow to hair.

Make boy's hair in same way, drawing a 20 cm (8 in) diameter circle and cutting off a 2·5 cm (1 in) section (see diagram 3).

Dolls' clothes

Notes: The seam allowance is 5 mm ($\frac{1}{4}$ in) on all pieces unless otherwise stated. Hems and all casings for elastic are turned 5 mm ($\frac{1}{4}$ in) then 1 cm ($\frac{3}{8}$ in). Join all pieces with right sides facing. Use either buttons or snap fasteners for fastening the garments.

Girl's pants and underskirt

You will need: 50 cm ($\frac{5}{8}$ yd) of 91 cm (36 in) wide white cotton fabric; 1·40 m ($1\frac{5}{8}$ yd) of lace trimming about 2 cm ($\frac{3}{4}$ in) wide; 60 cm ($\frac{3}{4}$ yd) of narrow elastic; 3 buttons or snap fasteners.

To make pants: Cut two pieces from trouser pattern, placing fold line marked on pattern to fold in fabric each time. Hem lower edges of each piece to form casings for elastic. Sew lace trim to lower edge of each casing then thread 16 cm ($6\frac{1}{4}$ in) of elastic through, securing elastic in place at each end.

Join pants pieces at centre edges then bring these seams together and join inside leg edges. Hem waist edge and thread through a 24 cm ($9\frac{1}{2}$ in) length of elastic.

To make underskirt: Trace off bodice pattern and mark dotted lines at neck, arm-hole and side edges. Cut out pattern on dotted lines.

Cut out one bodice front piece, placing fold edge of pattern to fold in fabric. Cut out two back pieces. Join front to back pieces at side

73

edges. For a lining make another bodice in same way. Join both pieces round all edges, leaving shoulder and lower edges open. Clip curves in seams and turn bodice right side out. Turn in raw edges at shoulders and press, then slip stitch front and back shoulder edges together.

For skirt cut a fabric strip 24 by 91 cm (9½ by 36 in). Narrowly hem one long edge and sew on lace trim. Make two 5 mm (¼ in) tucks at 1 cm (⅜ in) intervals above hem edge. Join short edges of skirt pieces, taking 1 cm (⅜ in) seam and leaving a gap about 8 cm (3 in) at top of seam for back opening. Press seam open then stitch down turnings on the gap.

Gather upper edge of skirt to fit lower edge of bodice. Join gathered top of skirt to bodice then turn in lower raw edge of bodice lining and slip stitch it over seam. Sew on fastenings at back of bodice.

Girl's dress

You will need: 50 cm (⅝ yd) of 91 cm (36 in) wide fabric; 1·30 m (1½ yd) of narrow ric-rac braid; 24 cm (9½ in) of narrow elastic; 3 buttons or snap fasteners.

To make: Using bodice pattern cut one front piece, placing pattern to fold in fabric where shown, and two back pieces. Join them at sides and shoulders. Make another bodice in same way for lining. Join lining to bodice round neck and back edges. Clip curves in seam, turn right side out and press; tack raw edges of armholes together.

Cut two sleeves, placing fold edge shown on pattern to fold in fabric each time. Make two 5 mm (¼ in) tucks across each sleeve, the first one where shown on pattern and the second about 1·5 cm (⅝ in) below it. Sew ric-rac below second tuck. Join underarm edges of each sleeve. Hem lower edges of sleeves and thread 12 cm (4¾ in) of elastic through each one.

Run a gathering thread along armhole edge of each sleeve where shown on pattern. Pin armhole edges of sleeves into armholes of bodice, matching underarm and sleeve seams and pulling up gathers at tops of sleeves to fit. Sew sleeves in place. Clip seams at curves; oversew raw edges.

For dress skirt cut a fabric strip 26 cm by 91 cm (10¼ by 36 in). Make two tucks as for sleeves – the first about 6 cm (2⅜ in) from one long raw edge. Sew on ric-rac. Hem lower edge; complete as for underskirt.

Girl's apron

You will need: 1·10 m (1¼ yd) of 20·5 cm (8 in) wide broderie Anglaise edging fabric.

To make: For the skirt cut a fabric strip 16 by 78 cm (6¼ by 30¾ in), using broderie edging as one long edge. Hem short ends.

For waistband cut a fabric strip 4 by 28 cm (1½ by 11 in). Fold it in half along length, sew across short ends, turn right side out and press. Gather upper edge of skirt and sew to one long edge of band; turn in and sew remaining edge of band over seam. Make and sew fabric ties to ends of band.

For each shoulder strap cut a plain strip 4 by 14 cm (1½ by 5½ in), and a broderie Anglaise edging 4 by 16 cm (1½ by 6¼ in). Hem short ends of edging and gather to 12 cm (4¾ in). Sew edging centrally to one long edge of strip; sew other long edge of strip over seam.

Place skirt of apron round doll over the dress and tie at centre back. Place a shoulder strap over each shoulder and pin each end in place under waistband, leaving trimming free. Sew straps in place as pinned.

Boy's shirt

You will need: 20 cm (¼ yd) of 91 cm (36 in) wide fabric and a scrap of contrast fabric for bias collar and cuff strips; a scrap of ribbon; 4 buttons or snap fasteners.

To make: Add 5 cm (2 in) to lower edge of bodice pattern and trim 1 cm (⅜ in) off neck edge. Cut out bodice front and backs from this pattern as for girl's bodice. Join side and shoulder seams. Make another bodice in same way for lining. Join lining to bodice round back and lower edges, turn right side out and press.

Cut a 4 by 22 cm (1½ by 8¾ in) bias strip of fabric for neckband. Bind raw neck edges with this strip, stretching the strip to fit as it is sewn in place.

Cut two sleeves, shortening length to the line shown on sleeve pattern. Cut two 4 by 14 cm (1½ by 5½ in) bias strips of fabric for cuffs. Sew one long edge of each strip to lower edge of each sleeve, stretching strips to fit as they are sewn in place. Join underarm edges of sleeves then turn in remaining raw edges of bias strips and slip stitch in place over seams.

Set sleeves into bodice armholes as before. Sew a ribbon bow to front of neckband and fastenings to back edges.

Trousers

You will need: A small piece of fabric for trousers and thin fabric for lining; 2 buttons and 2 snap fasteners.

To make: Cut two trouser pieces from fabric, cutting leg length as shown on pattern. Make

as for girl's pants, omitting elastic and lace trim in hemmed waist and lower edges.

For shoulder straps cut two 6 by 25 cm (2⅜ by 9¾ in) fabric strips. Join long edges of each strip and across one short end. Turn right side out and press. Place the remaining raw edge of each strap inside back edge of pants on each side of centre seam. Sew these ends in place at an angle so straps will cross over at back before passing over shoulders.

Make lining as for pants using thin fabric, but do *not* hem upper and lower edges. Place lining inside pants, wrong sides facing, and slip stitch upper edge and lower leg edges to pants, making slightly larger turnings on lining so it does not show on right side. Sew snap fasteners to fasten strap ends, sew buttons to outside of pants at same position.

For underpants use trouser pattern, cutting leg shorter as shown. Make as for girl's pants, omitting lace trim.

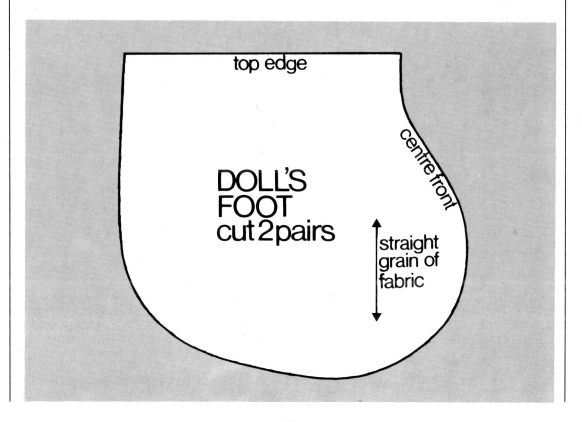

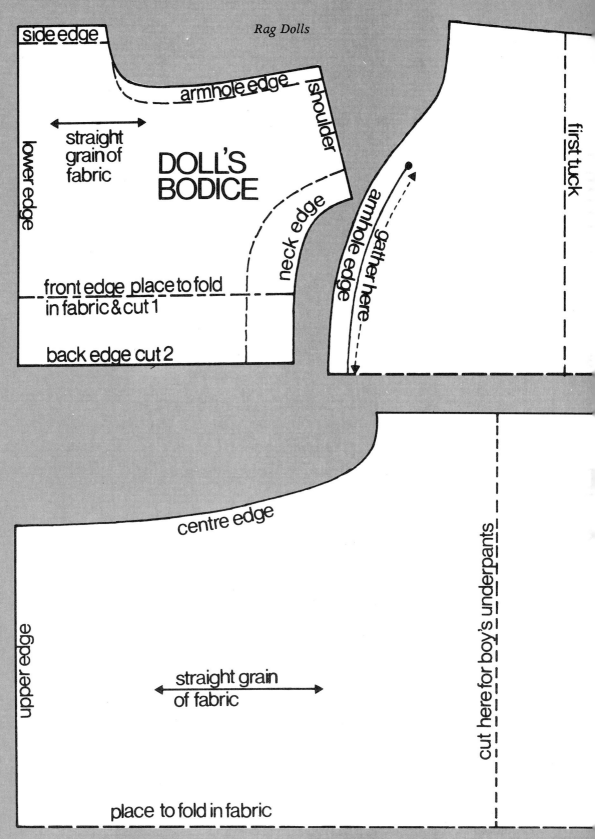

side edge

armhole edge

shoulder

straight
grain of
fabric

DOLL'S
BODICE

lower edge

neck edge

armhole edge

gather here

first tuck

front edge place to fold
in fabric & cut 1

back edge cut 2

centre edge

upper edge

straight grain
of fabric

cut here for boy's underpants

place to fold in fabric

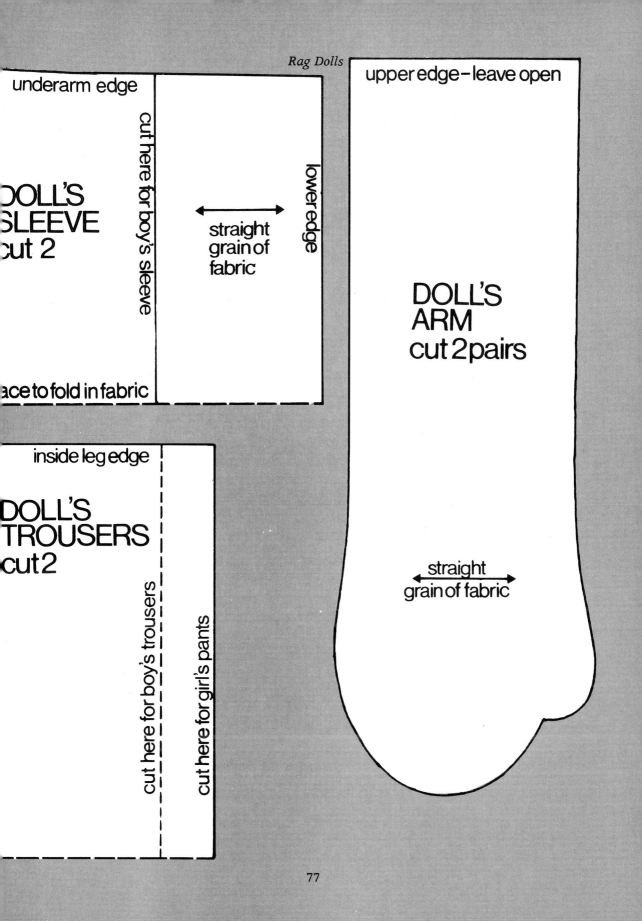

underarm edge

DOLL'S SLEEVE cut 2

cut here for boy's sleeve

lower edge

straight grain of fabric

...ace to fold in fabric

upper edge – leave open

DOLL'S ARM cut 2 pairs

straight grain of fabric

inside leg edge

DOLL'S TROUSERS cut 2

cut here for boy's trousers

cut here for girl's pants

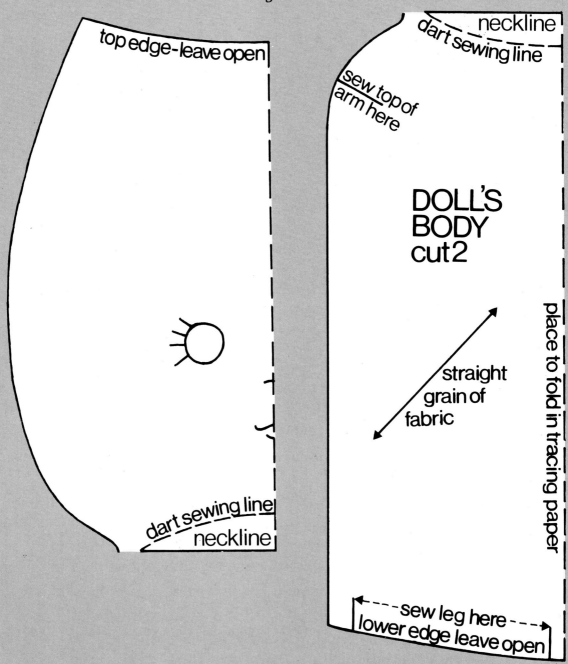

top edge-leave open

neckline

dart sewing line

sew top of
arm here

**DOLL'S
BODY
cut 2**

straight
grain of
fabric

place to fold in tracing paper

dart sewing line
neckline

sew leg here
lower edge leave open

The Adaptable Rag Doll

You can use the same, easy method to make these three 46-cm (18-in) high rag dolls. One is a dressing-up doll (with removable clothes). The second is a pretty nightdress case. The third is a topsy-turvy doll based on a popular nursery rhyme

For the doll you will need: Stockinette (the kind sold in rolls for household cleaning and polishing cars which can be bought in rolls in Woolworths, supermarkets and car accessory shops. It is about 22 cm (8¾ in) wide, and one large roll is enough to make three dolls; about 113 g (¼ lb) of stuffing; a small ball of thick-knit yarn; scraps of black felt, red pencil; black and red thread for face; white tape; adhesive.

Note: Take 1 cm (⅜ in) seams, except where stated otherwise.

Dressing-up doll

For the body and head cut a 30 cm (12 in) length off the stockinette roll. Fold it in half bringing side edges of roll together and join these edges. Gather one end of the tube, pull up gathers and fasten them securely (this will be the top of the head). Turn right side out and insert stuffing, to make a sausage shape measuring about 28 cm (11 in) around. Turn in and oversew remaining raw edges (see diagram 1).

To make the neck, tie a length of tape very tightly round the shape, 13 cm (5 in) down from top of head. Cut the tape ends short and sew them into back of neck.

For eyes, cut two 1 cm (⅜ in) diameter circles of black felt and glue them in place 5 cm (2 in) up from neck and 2·5 cm (1 in) apart. Work eyelashes in black thread. Use red thread to work a small straight stitch for mouth, 2 cm (¾ in) below eyes.

Moisten the point of red pencil and rub a little colour over cheeks. Blend colour into cheeks by rubbing with a piece of wet cloth.

For hair, wind yarn three times round two fingers, then sew these loops to head, beginning at one side of head. Continue making loops and sewing them in place across forehead to the other side of head. (The hat will cover the rest of the head.)

For each leg, cut a 24 cm (9½ in) length of stockinette. Fold it in half to bring the side edges of the roll together, then fold in half again (see diagram 2) and sew all the 24 cm (9½ in) edges together taking a 5 mm (¼ in) seam. Continue the seam round one end as

shown in diagram 2. Trim off corners and turn right side out. Stuff the leg until it measures 13 cm (5 in) around. Turn in and oversew remaining raw edges then sew leg to lower edge of body.

For each arm, cut a 19 cm (7½ in) length of stockinette. Make as for legs, but take a 1 cm (⅜ in) seam. Stuff arm to measure 11 cm (4¼ in) around, leaving 4 cm (1½ in) at top unstuffed. Turn in and oversew raw edges; sew an arm to each side of body, 2·5 cm (1 in) down from neck. For wrist tie thread round, 5 cm (2 in) from end of arm.

Doll's clothes

For patterns, copy the outlines shown on diagram square by square, on to metric graph paper (each square on diagram equals 1 cm). Join all fabrics with right sides facing.

Shoes

You will need: Scraps of felt.

To make: Cut four shoe pieces from pattern; on two of them cut out shape shown by dotted line on pattern. Join shoe pieces in pairs round curved edges, taking 5 mm (¼ in) seam. Turn right side out, fit shoes on doll's legs and sew in place.

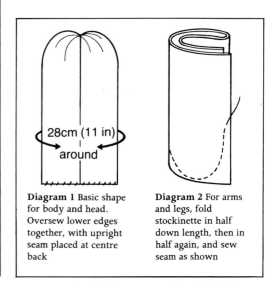

Diagram 1 Basic shape for body and head. Oversew lower edges together, with upright seam placed at centre back

Diagram 2 For arms and legs, fold stockinette in half down length, then in half again, and sew seam as shown

Pantaloons

You will need: 25 cm ($9\frac{3}{4}$ in) of 91 cm (36 in) wide fabric (this fabric is also used for neck and cuff bindings on the dress); elastic and lace trimming.

To make: Cut two pantaloon pieces, placing edge of pattern indicated to fold in fabric. Join pieces at centre seams; clip seams at curves. Hem lower leg edges and sew on trimming. Join inside leg edges. Hem waist edge, taking a 1 cm ($\frac{3}{8}$ in) turning twice, then thread through elastic.

Dress

You will need: 30 cm (12 in) of 91 cm (36 in) wide fabric; fabric oddments left from pantaloons for contrast edging; 2 snap fasteners.

To make: Cut one front, two backs and two sleeves as directed on the pattern. Join centre back edges of back pieces to within 14 cm ($5\frac{1}{2}$ in) of neck edge. Press seam open and stitch down remaining raw edges. Join armhole edges of sleeves to front and back of dress and clip curves.

Gather the lower edges of sleeves to fit doll's arms loosely, then bind them with 4 cm ($1\frac{1}{2}$ in) wide bias strips of contrast fabric. Gather neck edge to fit neck and bind this in same way. Join sides of dress and sleeves; hem lower edge. Sew snap fasteners to back opening.

Pinafore and hat

You will need: 55 cm ($21\frac{1}{2}$ in) of 91 cm (36 in) wide fabric; ribbon for the hat band.

To make pinafore: Cut a fabric strip 18 by 91 cm (7 by 36 in). Gather one long edge to measure 26 cm ($10\frac{1}{4}$ in), hem other edges.

For waistband cut a fabric strip 5 by 68 cm (2 by $26\frac{3}{4}$ in); bind gathered edge of pinafore with this, leaving an equal portion of waistband at each side for ties.

For each shoulder strap cut a fabric strip 5 by 15 cm (2 by 6 in). Join long edges of each strip and turn right side out. Sew ends of shoulder straps to inside of waistband.

To make hat: Cut two 30 cm (12 in) diameter circles of fabric. Join them round edges, taking 5 mm ($\frac{1}{4}$ in) seam and leaving a gap for turning. Turn right side out, slip stitch opening. Gather round hat 4 cm ($1\frac{1}{2}$ in) from edge, pull up gathers to fit doll's head behind hair, and fasten off. Put a little stuffing in hat, then sew it to head all round. Sew ribbon over gathers.

Nightdress-case doll

You will need: Stockinette, yarn etc. as for making the dressing-up doll.

For her clothes: 50 cm ($19\frac{1}{2}$ in) of 91 cm (36 in) wide fabric; contrast fabric for hat and apron; oddment of fabric for the case lining; 5 snap fasteners; 1·20 m ($1\frac{3}{8}$ yd) of lace edging.

To make the doll: For the body and head, cut a 26 cm ($10\frac{1}{4}$ in) length of stockinette. Sew, stuff and slip stitch lower edges, then make neck and face, as for dressing-up doll.

For fringe, wind yarn twice round two fingers and stitch loops to centre of doll's forehead.

For hair, wind yarn three times round a 24 cm ($9\frac{1}{2}$ in) piece of card, slip yarn off the card and sew centre of strands above fringe then sew loops to each side of the doll's head as shown in illustration.

Her clothes

Make the hat as for dressing-up doll. For dress bodice, cut a fabric strip 8 by 30 cm (3 by 12 in). Join short edges, and turn right side out. Place bodice on doll. Turn in raw edge at neck, place lace edging round the turned-in edge and run a gathering thread round through lace and fabric. Pull up gathers round neck and fasten off. Turn in remaining raw edge at waist and slip stitch it to doll's body.

Make arms as for dressing-up doll but stuff them only halfway up. Trim 1 cm ($\frac{3}{8}$ in) off upper edge of each arm and oversew raw edges together, pulling stitches to gather. For each sleeve cut a fabric strip 16 by 17 cm ($6\frac{1}{4}$ by $6\frac{3}{4}$ in). Join short edges, turn right side out and slip a sleeve over each arm. Turn in wrist edge, add lace and gather as for neck of

bodice. Turn in top edge of each sleeve and oversew, pulling stitches to gather. Sew top of a sleeve each side of doll, 2 cm ($\frac{3}{4}$ in) down from neck.

For case lining, cut a fabric strip 28 by 72 cm (11 by 28$\frac{1}{2}$ in) and join short edges. Hem one remaining raw edge then gather the other edge to fit round doll's waist and sew it, through the gathers, over the waist edge of the bodice all round. Sew snap fasteners to the lower edge of case.

For the skirt, cut a fabric strip 30 by 91 cm (12 by 36 in). Join the short edges, hem lower edge and sew on lace trim, then gather the waist edge. Sew skirt round waist on top of the case lining.

For the apron, cut a fabric piece 18 by 24 cm (7 by 9$\frac{1}{2}$ in). Gather one long edge and hem remaining raw edges. Sew gathered edge to waist. For apron waistband, cut a strip of matching fabric 4 cm (1$\frac{1}{2}$ in) wide; turn in and press raw edges then sew strip round doll's waist to cover all raw fabric edges at waist.

Topsy-turvy doll

> There was a little girl, who had a little curl
> Right in the middle of her forehead.
> When she was good she was very, very good,
> But when she was bad she was horrid!

You will need: Stockinette, yarn etc. as for the dressing-up doll.

For her clothes: 50 cm (19$\frac{1}{2}$ in) of 91 cm (36 in) wide fabric for each end of doll; pieces of contrast fabric for hats and belts; 2·30 m (2$\frac{1}{2}$ yd) of lace edging or trimming.

The doll

For her body and both heads, cut a 38 cm (15 in) length of stockinette. Join long edges, turn and stuff as for the dressing-up doll. Gather the remaining raw edges, turn them in and fasten off securely. Tie tapes tightly round the sausage shape, 13 cm (5$\frac{1}{8}$ in) away from each gathered end, to form each neck.

Make smiling face as for dressing-up doll, stitching a V-shape for smiling mouth. For the scowling face, cut a little off the top of each eye and instead of eyelashes work a single black stitch across top of each eye. Work an inverted V-shape for sulky mouth.

For each 'curl', twist a yarn strand until it curls up tightly, then sew a curl to each forehead. Make hair as for nightdress case.

Her clothes

For each dress bodice, cut a fabric strip 8 by 30 cm (3 by 12 in). Join the strips at one long edge, taking a 5 mm ($\frac{1}{4}$ in) seam. Join short edges, then fit bodice on doll and gather and trim both neck edges as for nightdress case.

Make four arms and sleeves in the same

way as for the nightdress case.

For each skirt, cut a fabric strip 30 by 91 cm (12 by 36 in). Join short edges of each strip then place them right sides together and join one long edge, at the same time enclosing a strip of lace edging between the seam so the edging will extend below lower edge of skirt when turned right side out. Turn skirt right side out, bringing raw edges together; press.

Gather each remaining raw edge separately to fit round doll's waist. Place one gathered edge round seam at doll's waist (making sure

the skirt fabric matches bodice fabric) then back stitch skirt to doll through gathers all round. Turn doll the other way up and back stitch the remaining skirt in place in same way. To cover raw edges of skirts cut a 4 cm (1½ in) wide strip of contrast fabric, turn in and press raw edges then sew each band round waist.

For each hat cut two 22 cm (8¾ in) diameter circles of contrast fabric. Make each hat as for dressing-up doll, but omit the stuffing and gather 2·5 cm (1 in) from edge.

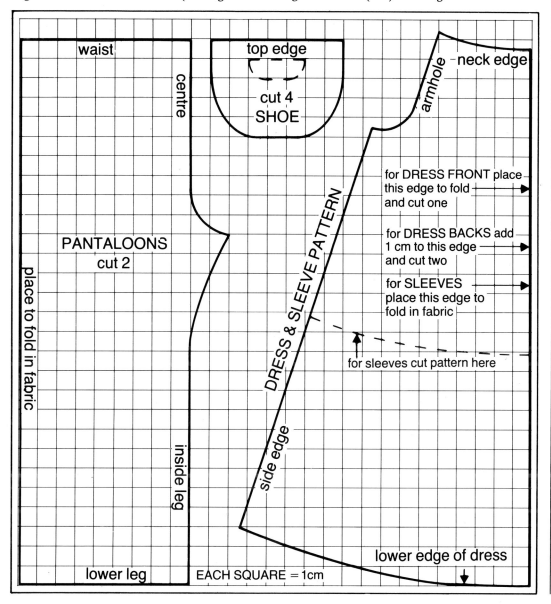

The Well-dressed Doll

*This charming rag doll stands just 25 cm (10 in) tall and has a wardrobe of five pretty
outfits. She would make a perfect playmate for any little girl who loves clothes*

For the doll you will need: Small pieces of
pink cotton fabric; fur fabric for hair; white
and black felt; pink and red thread; red
pencil; a small amount of stuffing; adhesive.

For the clothes: Scraps of fabrics and
trimmings; narrow elastic; lace edging; felt;
small snap fasteners.

Notes: Trace off all the pattern pieces onto
paper. Where patterns have a dot and dash
edge, fold the paper in half and place the fold
over this line. Trace off the outline then cut
out through both layers of paper. Open up to
give full-size patterns.

Cut out all pieces following the directions
on the patterns.

Join all pieces with right sides facing; take
5 mm ($\frac{1}{4}$ in) seams unless otherwise stated.

The doll

To make head and body: Cut two body
pieces from pink fabric. Mark the face on the
right side of one piece then make neck darts
on wrong side of both pieces. Join body
pieces round edges leaving a gap in the seam
at the lower edge as indicated on the pattern.
Trim seam and turn body right side out. Stuff
head firmly then stuff body. Ladder stitch
gap in seam. Work nose in pink satin stitch.
Work mouth in small back stitches using red
thread, then work back, oversewing through
each stitch. Cut eyes from black felt and stick
in place. Colour cheeks by rubbing with red
pencil.

Cut two hair pieces from fur fabric with
smooth stroke of fur in direction shown on
pattern. Join pieces round outer edges then
turn in remaining raw edges a little and slip
stitch. Pull hair on head to fit neatly then slip
stitch to head all round. Sew small ribbon bow
to hair.

To make legs: For legs cut two 8 by 9 cm
($3\frac{1}{8}$ by $3\frac{1}{2}$ in) pieces of pink fabric. Cut two
pairs of sock pieces from white felt. Join sock
pieces in pairs for about 2 cm ($\frac{3}{4}$ in) down
front seam, press seam open then join upper
edges of sock pieces to one short edge of each
leg piece. Trim seam then join remainder of
sock pieces round outer edges and join 9 cm
($3\frac{1}{2}$ in) edges of leg pieces. Trim seams round
socks then turn legs right side out and stuff.
Turn in upper edges of legs and slip stitch
then sew to front of body about 1 cm ($\frac{3}{8}$ in)
away from lower body seam.

Cut two pairs of shoe pieces from felt as
directed on pattern and cut two 5 mm by
4 cm ($\frac{1}{4}$ by $1\frac{1}{2}$ in) strips of felt for shoe straps.
Join shoe pieces in pairs round outer edges.
Trim seams and turn right side out. Put shoes
on feet and place straps in position as illustrated tucking ends of straps in shoes at each
side, then sew shoes and straps to feet.

To make arms: Cut two pairs of arm pieces
from pink fabric. Join them in pairs round
edges leaving top edges open. Trim seams
round hands, turn right side out and stuff to
within 3 cm ($1\frac{1}{4}$ in) of top. Turn in top edges,
bring seams together then make small
inverted pleats as shown in diagram 1.
Oversew all edges together then sew an arm
to each side of body 5 mm ($\frac{1}{4}$ in) down from
neck.

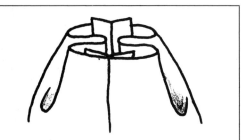

Diagram 1 Make one inverted pleat at either side
of each arm

The clothes

Panties

Cut out two panty pieces and hem lower edges taking 5 mm ($\frac{1}{4}$ in) turnings twice to form casings for elastic. Sew narrow lace trimming to lower edges. Thread elastic through casings to fit legs and secure at each end with a stitch or two. Join pieces at centre front and back edges clipping curves in seams. Join at inside leg edges. Hem waist edge as for lower edges and thread through elastic to fit waist.

Nightdress

Cut out one pair of back bodice pieces and one front bodice cutting lower edges of pieces by dotted line indicated. Cut two long sleeves as shown on sleeve pattern. Cut a 2 by 14 cm ($\frac{3}{4}$ by 5$\frac{1}{2}$ in) bias strip of fabric for binding neck edge. Sew ric-rac or trimming to bodice front as illustrated. Join front bodice to backs at shoulders. Run gathering threads along tops of sleeves as shown on pattern. Tack armhole edges of sleeves to armhole edges of bodice matching points A to shoulder seams and pulling up gathering threads on sleeves to fit. Sew seams as tacked then clip curves. Turn in lower edges of sleeves 5 mm ($\frac{1}{4}$ in) twice and stitch, forming casings, for elastic. Thread elastic through to fit wrists and secure at each end of casings with a stitch or two. Turn in back edges of bodice 5 mm ($\frac{1}{4}$ in) twice and stitch. Bind neck edge with bias strip, clipping curves. Now join side edges of bodice and underarm edges of sleeves to complete top of nightdress.

For skirt, cut a 16 by 30 cm (6$\frac{1}{4}$ by 12 in) strip of fabric. Sew trimming parallel to and 3 cm (1$\frac{1}{4}$ in) away from one long edge – this will be the hem edge. Join the short edges from hem taking 1 cm ($\frac{3}{8}$ in) seam and leaving 4 cm (1$\frac{1}{2}$ in) open at top of seam. Press seam to one side then turn in raw edges of seam and stitch to neaten. Hem lower edge of skirt then gather upper edge to fit lower edge of bodice. Sew gathered edge of skirt to bodice. To finish off the nightdress, sew ribbon bow to the front and three snap fasteners to back edges.

Short red dress

Make as for nightdress cutting short sleeves as indicated on pattern. Make short skirt as for nightdress using a 9 by 34 cm (3$\frac{1}{2}$ by 13$\frac{1}{2}$ in) strip of fabric. To complete the dress, sew lace edging to the hem edge.

Frilled pop-over

Cut one pair of back pieces and one front piece as directed on pattern. Join front to backs at side edges then turn in shoulder edges 5 mm ($\frac{1}{4}$ in) and press. Cut a 45 cm (17$\frac{3}{4}$ in) length of 4 cm (1$\frac{1}{2}$ in) wide lace edging for frill. Gather lace to fit round lower edge of pop-over between points A on the back pieces. Sew gathered edge of lace in position with right sides facing and raw edges level. Cut out and make lining in the same way as for pop-over omitting frill. Place lining and pop-over together and join round front neck and back neck edges, armholes and centre back edges. Clip curves in seams and turn pop-over right side out pushing shoulder edges through with a knitting needle. Slip stitch front shoulder edges of pop-over and lining to back shoulder edges. Turn in and slip stitch lower edge of lining over frill seam. Sew narrow lace edging round neck edge and round frill seam then sew a snap fastener to back neck edges.

Flowery blouse

Make bodice as for nightdress bodice cutting lower edges by line indicated on pattern and using short sleeve pattern. Hem lower edges of sleeves and omit elastic.

Felt pop-over

Cut two backs and one front as directed on pattern trimming away side edges as indicated. Trim 5 mm ($\frac{1}{4}$ in) off all neck and armhole edges. Cut two pockets using pocket pattern. Stitch pockets to front as shown on pattern. Join front to backs at shoulders then trim seams. On right side of pop-over, top-stitch all round neck and armhole edges as illustrated. Join side seams then top-stitch all round back and lower edges. Sew snap fasteners to back edges.

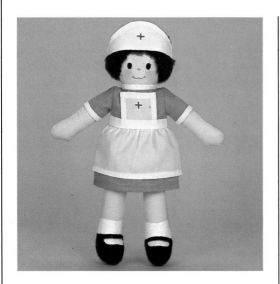

Nurse's outfit

Use pale blue fabric for the dress. Cut bodice front and backs using bodice pattern and cutting lower edges by line indicated. Cut two sleeves using nurse's sleeve pattern. For skirt, cut a 9 by 26 cm ($3\frac{1}{2}$ by $10\frac{1}{4}$ in) strip of fabric. Make as for nightdress but instead of gathering sleeve tops, ease them into arm-holes. Omit elastic in lower edges of sleeves and, instead, bind with a 2 cm ($\frac{3}{4}$ in) wide bias strip of white fabric. Bind neck edge.

For apron skirt cut a 7 by 24 cm ($2\frac{3}{4}$ by $9\frac{1}{2}$ in) strip of white fabric. Take narrow hems on all edges except for one long edge. Gather this edge to measure 16 cm ($6\frac{1}{4}$ in); then bind this edge with a 3 by 20 cm ($1\frac{1}{4}$ by 8 in) bias strip of white fabric, with the skirt placed centrally so an equal portion of band extends at each side for the back overlap. For apron bib, cut a 6 cm ($2\frac{3}{8}$ in) square of fabric. Narrowly hem all raw edges then slip one edge behind waistband at front and slip stitch in position. Sew a snap fastener to back waistband overlap and halves of two snaps to top corners of bib. Sew other halves of snaps to dress front to hold bib in position. Use ball point pen to mark red cross on bib.

Cut cap as directed on pattern. Join raw edges leaving one short straight edge open. Turn cap right side out then turn in and slip stitch opening. Top-stitch cap round edges and sew a 10 cm (4 in) strip of narrow elastic to short edges. Mark on red cross.

Scottish dance dress

Note that the skirt and blouse are sewn together for ease in dressing the doll. Make bodice as for short dress with puffed sleeves, using white fabric and trimming neck and sleeve edges with narrow lace edging. Make a pattern for circular skirt as follows: draw and cut out a 20 cm (8 in) diameter circle of paper then draw and cut a 6 cm ($2\frac{3}{8}$ in) diameter circle from the centre and discard it. The inner edge of the pattern is the waist edge and the outer edge is the hem. Cut one skirt piece from checked fabric then make a cut from hem to waist edge for back opening. Join these edges from hem to waist taking a 1 cm ($\frac{3}{8}$ in) seam and leaving a 4 cm ($1\frac{1}{2}$ in) gap at the top of the seam. Finish this opening as for the short dress. Run a gathering thread round the waist edge and pull up gathers to fit lower edge of bodice then sew in place. Hem lower edge of skirt then sew snap fasteners to back edges.

For black felt bodice, cut one pair of fronts and one pair of backs as directed on felt bodice pattern. Join fronts to backs at shoulders and sides oversewing edges together neatly. Turn right side out and use needle and thin cord to lace front edges together as illustrated, tying cord in a bow at top. Sew snap fasteners to back.

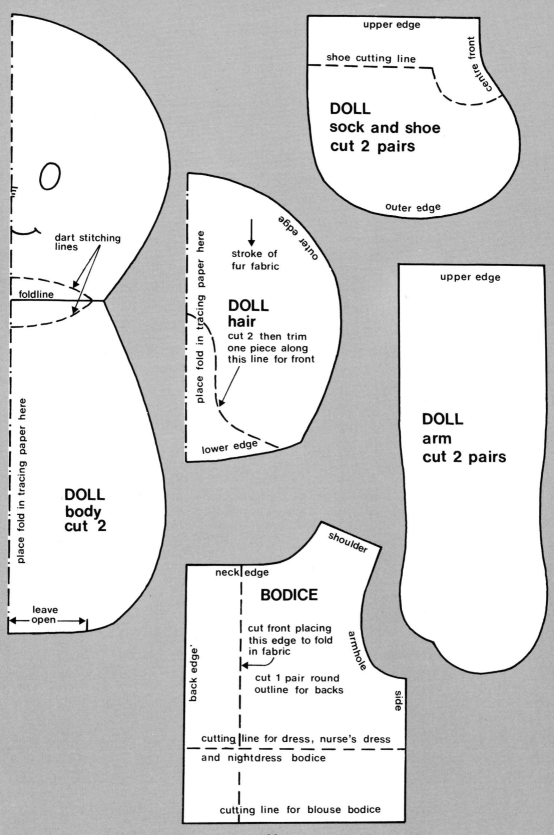

DOLL
sock and shoe
cut 2 pairs

upper edge

shoe cutting line

centre front

outer edge

dart stitching lines

foldline

place fold in tracing paper here

DOLL
body
cut 2

leave open

stroke of fur fabric

place fold in tracing paper here

outer edge

DOLL
hair

cut 2 then trim one piece along this line for front

lower edge

upper edge

DOLL
arm
cut 2 pairs

shoulder

neck edge

BODICE

cut front placing this edge to fold in fabric

back edge'

cut 1 pair round outline for backs

armhole

side

cutting line for dress, nurse's dress and nightdress bodice

cutting line for blouse bodice

88

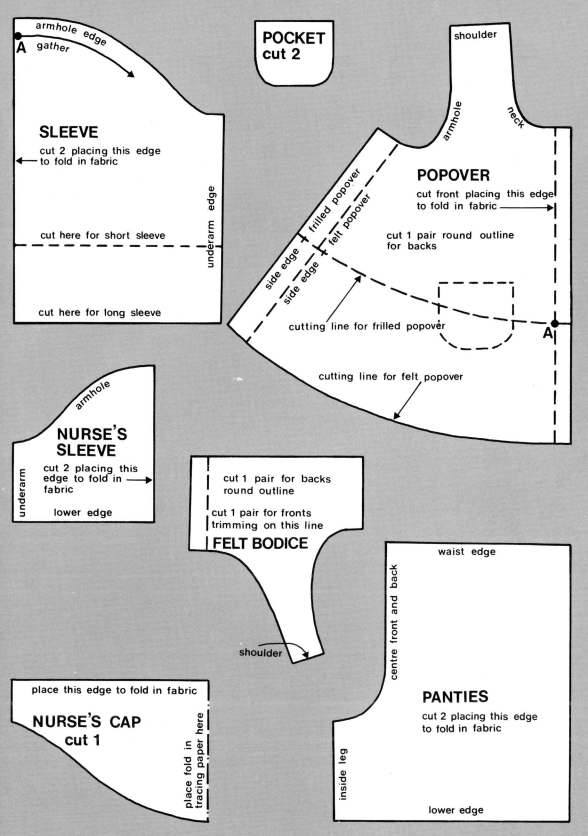

SLEEVE
cut 2 placing this edge to fold in fabric

armhole edge

A gather

cut here for short sleeve

cut here for long sleeve

underarm edge

POCKET cut 2

shoulder

armhole

neck

POPOVER
cut front placing this edge to fold in fabric

cut 1 pair round outline for backs

frilled popover
felt popover

side edge

side edge

cutting line for frilled popover

A

cutting line for felt popover

NURSE'S SLEEVE
cut 2 placing this edge to fold in fabric

armhole

underarm

lower edge

cut 1 pair for backs round outline

cut 1 pair for fronts trimming on this line

FELT BODICE

shoulder

place this edge to fold in fabric

NURSE'S CAP cut 1

place fold in tracing paper here

waist edge

centre front and back

PANTIES
cut 2 placing this edge to fold in fabric

inside leg

lower edge

89

Glad-rag Doll

This beautiful, 50-cm (20-in) rag doll can be made almost entirely without patterns. Simply cut out and sew up tubes of stretchy fabric, tying thread round to shape the neck and wrists. Patterns and instructions are supplied for four smart outfits to suit every occasion!

For the doll you will need: 50 cm ($\frac{5}{8}$ yd) of cotton stockinette – tubular knit 57 cm (22$\frac{1}{2}$ in) wide, opening out to 114 cm (45 in) width (note that this amount will make two dolls). Alternatively you can use an old, plain T-shirt or vest; 300 g (10 oz) of stuffing; scraps of brown felt, white and red thread; a red pencil for colouring cheeks and nose; a large ball of chunky knitting yarn; bias binding to match stockinette, (for sewing hair in place); adhesive.

Notes: Cut out all stockinette pieces with most stretch (i.e. the width of the fabric) going across *width* of pieces, as shown by arrows on diagrams and patterns. Take 5 mm ($\frac{1}{4}$ in) seams on all pieces, stretching the fabric slightly as it is stitched to prevent stitching from snapping when the pieces are stuffed.

The doll

To make body and head: Cut two stockinette pieces 9 by 35 cm (3$\frac{1}{2}$ by 13$\frac{3}{4}$ in), with most stretch going across the 9 cm (3$\frac{1}{2}$ in) width. Mark a faint line across one piece for neckline, 17 cm (6$\frac{3}{4}$ in) down from one short edge.

Join the pieces as shown on diagram 1, curving the stitching about 2 cm ($\frac{3}{4}$ in) into neckline, rounding off corners at the lower edge of body and leaving top edges open. Trim seam at neck and lower corners, then turn right side out and stuff firmly.

Using strong thread, run a gathering thread round top of head 1 cm ($\frac{3}{8}$ in) from raw edge. Pull up gathers tightly, turning in raw edges, then fasten off oversewing securely. Using doubled sewing thread, wind thread round neckline several times, pulling tightly, to form the neck. Knot threads and sew thread ends into doll.

To make legs: For each leg, cut a 10 by 23 cm (4 by 9 in) piece of stockinette, with most stretch going across the 10 cm (4 in) width. Cut four upper foot pieces from pattern and join them in pairs at centre front edges. Trim seams. Join upper edge of each pair of foot pieces to one 10 cm (4 in) edge of each leg piece. Now join centre back edges of foot uppers and the long edges of each leg.

Cut two foot soles from pattern and tack them to the lower edges of each upper foot, matching points A and B. Stitch seams as tacked then trim them. Turn legs right side out and stuff firmly to within 3 cm (1$\frac{1}{4}$ in) of upper edges. Turn in upper edges 1 cm ($\frac{3}{8}$ in) and oversew, then sew them securely to lower edge of body.

To make arms: For each arm, cut a piece of stockinette 8 by 24 cm (3 by 9$\frac{1}{2}$ in), with most stretch going across the 8 cm (3 in) width. Fold each piece and stitch as shown in diagram 2, rounding off corners for hand at one end; trim off corners. Turn right side out and stuff firmly to within 5 cm (2 in) at top edges. Turn in raw edges 1 cm ($\frac{3}{8}$ in) and oversew, pulling stitches to gather slightly.

Sew an arm securely to each side of body, 2·5 cm (1 in) down from neck. Tie thread tightly round wrists 6 cm (2$\frac{3}{8}$ in) from ends of arms as for neck.

For the face: Lightly mark a shallow U-shape for the mouth, 3 cm (1$\frac{1}{4}$ in) up from neck, making it about 2·5 cm (1 in) wide. Work the mouth line in back stitch then work back along the line, oversewing through each stitch.

For the eyes, spread adhesive on back of a piece of brown felt and allow it to dry before

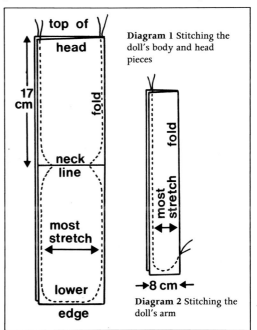

Diagram 1 Stitching the doll's body and head pieces

top of head

fold

17 cm

neck line

most stretch

lower edge

most stretch

fold

→8 cm←

Diagram 2 Stitching the doll's arm

cutting out eyes. Work a few white stitches on each eye for a highlight. Stick eyes in place about 3 cm (1¼ in) apart, with lower edges 5 cm (2 in) up from neck. Use red pencil to mark nose. Colour cheeks by rubbing fabric with red pencil.

For the hair: First make the fringe. Cut a 12 cm (4¾ in) length of binding. Wind yarn a few times round four fingers and stitch one end of loops to tape. Repeat right across to cover tape. Trim off other looped ends to make an even fringe. Sew tape across the doll's forehead (running from side to side), roughly 6 cm (2⅜ in) above eyes.

For rest of hair, cut 50 cm (19½ in) lengths of yarn, laying them side by side (see diagram 3) until they form a 14 cm (5½ in) width. Cut a 16 cm (6¼ in) length of binding, spread it with adhesive then place it across centre of strands. Leave until adhesive is dry, then stitch through centre of binding. Turn under ends of the binding and sew hair to centre parting of doll's head, with the binding against the head. To gather hair to each side of head, sew the centre of a length of yarn to the seam line at each side of head, level with mouth. Gather hair to each side then tie this strand tightly round to hold hair in bunches. Trim ends evenly.

The doll's clothes

Notes: The seam allowance is 1 cm (⅜ in) on all pieces unless stated otherwise. When the instructions say 'hem edge', take a 5 mm (¼ in) turning then a 1 cm (⅜ in) turning and press, then stitch in place. 'Narrowly hem' means taking 5 mm (¼ in) turnings twice. Join fabric with right sides facing. Press seams open after stitching unless stated otherwise.

All garments are made from the basic patterns given, altering patterns for each garment if necessary as directed.

Socks

You will need: One pair of baby socks.

To make: Place socks wrong side out on doll's feet, with top edges at the correct

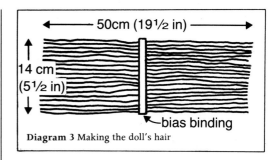

Diagram 3 Making the doll's hair

height for ankle socks. Place pins round the foot portion of each sock to make it fit closely round the doll's foot. Remove socks and stitch along the line formed by pins. Trim away excess, 5 mm (¼ in) from the stitching line, then turn socks right side out.

Pants and petticoat

You will need: 30 cm (⅜ yd) of 91 cm (36 in) wide fabric; a short length of narrow elastic; 1·70 m (1⅞ yd) of narrow lace edging; 3 snap fasteners; a scrap of narrow ribbon.

To make pants: Cut two pants pieces as directed on pattern and hem lower edges of each piece. Sew lace to hem edges. Join pieces together at centre edges and clip seams at curves. Thread elastic through each lower hemmed edge to fit doll's legs, and secure at each side with a stitch or two. Bring centre seams together and join inside leg edges of each leg, then trim seam. Hem waist edge and thread elastic through to fit doll's waist.

To make petticoat: Cut bodice front and backs as stated on patterns. Trim 5 mm (¼ in) off shoulder edges, side edges and back edges of bodice pieces. Join front bodice to backs at side edges and trim seams. Cut another set of bodice pieces for the lining and make exactly as for bodice. Join lining to bodice round armholes, neck and down back edges, leaving shoulder edges open. Trim all seams and corners and clip into curves. Turn bodice right side out and press. Now turn in raw edges of shoulders 5 mm (¼ in) and slip stitch front shoulders of bodice to back shoulders. Join shoulders of lining in same way.

For skirt, cut a strip of fabric 16 by 50 cm (6¼ by 19½ in). Join the short edges leaving 7 cm (2¾ in) open at top of seam for back opening. Press seam to one side and neaten raw edges of opening. Gather top edge of skirt to fit lower edge of bodice and sew it to bodice, leaving lining free. Turn in lower raw edge of lining and slip stitch it over seam. Hem lower edge of petticoat and sew on lace edging. Sew lace edging round neck and armhole edges. Add a small ribbon bow at neckline and sew snap fasteners to back bodice edges.

Ankle-strap shoes

You will need: Small pieces of felt, iron-on interfacing and bias binding; 2 small buttons.

To make: Iron the interfacing on to felt, then for each shoe cut out one pair of uppers and one sole from pattern. Join uppers at centre front edges, taking 5 mm ($\frac{1}{4}$ in) seams. Sew one edge of bias binding to top edge of each piece on right side. Turn binding to inside and press. Join centre back edges of shoe uppers, taking 5 mm ($\frac{1}{4}$ in) seam. Now slip stitch other edge of binding to inside of shoes. Pin soles to lower edges of shoes, matching points A and B. Back stitch soles in place 3 mm ($\frac{1}{8}$ in) from edges. Turn shoes right side out, fit them on doll and press sole seam to smooth it out.

For each ankle strap cut a strip of plain felt 2 by 17 cm ($\frac{3}{4}$ by $6\frac{3}{4}$ in), (without interfacing). Fold each in half, with long edges together, and press. Round off corners at each end of straps. Stitch all round close to edges of straps. Catch the centre of one long edge of each strap to centre back of shoe. Sew a button to one end of each strap and cut slits in other end to suit buttons.

Slip-on shoes

Follow directions for ankle-strap shoes, omitting the straps.

Slippers

Make as for slip-on shoes, adding a small flower or ribbon bow to fronts.

Party dress

You will need: 30 cm ($\frac{3}{8}$ yd) of 91 cm (36 in) wide fabric; 1·30 m ($1\frac{3}{8}$ yd) of trimming; 3 snap fasteners; 30 cm ($\frac{3}{8}$ yd) of narrow ribbon.

To make: Cut bodice and sleeve pieces as directed on patterns. For skirt, cut a strip of fabric 17 by 60 cm ($6\frac{3}{4}$ by $23\frac{1}{2}$ in).

Join bodice front to backs at shoulders, then hem back edges. Run gathering threads along armhole edges of sleeves between dots. Pull up gathers so that armhole edges of sleeves fit armhole edges of bodice. Sew sleeves to bodice. Stitch again, just within first line of stitching, then trim seams close to this stitching. Join side edges of bodice and underarm edges of sleeves. Bind neck edge with a 2 cm ($\frac{3}{4}$ in) wide bias-cut strip of fabric, taking 5 mm ($\frac{1}{4}$ in) turnings.

Join short edges of skirt strip, leaving 8 cm (3 in) open at top of seam for back opening. Neaten the raw edges of opening and press seam to one side. Gather top raw edge of skirt to fit lower edge of bodice, then sew in place. Narrowly hem lower edge of skirt and sew on trimming. Finish lower edges of sleeves in the same way. Sew trimming to bodice round back neck, then to form a V-point at front waistline (as shown in illustration). Sew ribbon bow to V-point as shown, then sew snap fasteners to back opening of bodice.

Jacket

You will need: 30 cm ($\frac{3}{8}$ yd) of 91 cm (36 in) wide quilted fabric; 2 m ($2\frac{1}{4}$ yd) of bias binding; 5 small buttons.

To alter patterns: Alter bodice pattern as follows – extend lower edge by 8 cm (3 in), trim 1 cm ($\frac{3}{8}$ in) off armhole edge and also 1·5 cm ($\frac{5}{8}$ in) off back edge. Extend the lower edge of sleeve pattern by 5 cm (2 in).

Notes: When making the jacket, take 5 mm ($\frac{1}{4}$ in) seams on all pieces instead of 1 cm ($\frac{3}{8}$ in). Note also that front bodice piece will form back of jacket, so that the buttoned opening will be at the front. Cut out all pieces using altered patterns.

To make: Cut two pockets from pattern. Bind raw edges with bias binding, then sew to jacket fronts as shown in illustration. Join seams and set in sleeves as for dress bodice,

noting that armhole edges of sleeves do not need to be gathered as they can be eased to fit armholes. Bind lower edges of sleeves. Round off jacket front edges at neck and lower edges. Now bind round neck, front and lower edges of jacket.

To make looped fastenings, fold a 25 cm (10 in) length of bias binding into three along its length to make a very narrow strip, then stitch down centre of strip. Cut five 5 cm (2 in) lengths, one for each loop, then fold each in half and sew raw edges to inside of bias binding on right front of jacket, spacing them out evenly. Sew buttons to left front of jacket, to correspond with loops.

Trousers

You will need: 30 cm ($\frac{3}{8}$ yd) of 91 cm (36 in) wide needlecord fabric; a short length of elastic.

To make: Extend lower edge of pants pattern by 17 cm ($6\frac{3}{4}$ in), then cut out pieces as directed. Join seams as for pants, omitting trim, and elastic in lower edges. Hem waist edge and thread through elastic to fit waist. Narrowly hem lower edges.

Nightdress

You will need: 50 cm ($\frac{5}{8}$ yd) of 91 cm (36 in) wide fabric 1 m ($1\frac{1}{8}$ yd) of lace trimming; 3 snap fasteners; narrow elastic.

To make: Trim 2 cm ($\frac{3}{4}$ in) off lower edge of bodice pattern and 1 cm ($\frac{3}{8}$ in) off neck edge. Extend lower edge of sleeve pattern by 8 cm (3 in). Cut out bodice and sleeve pieces using the altered patterns.

Stitch three rows of trimming down front of bodice as shown in the illustration. Make bodice and sleeves and bind neck as for party dress, but hem lower edges of sleeves and thread elastic through to fit wrists.

For skirt cut a 30 by 60 cm ($11\frac{3}{4}$ by $23\frac{1}{2}$ in) fabric strip. Make and sew to bodice as for dress, sewing trimming to lower edge. Sew snap fasteners to back opening edges of bodice.

Short-sleeved blouse

You will need: 20 cm ($\frac{1}{4}$ yd) of 91 cm (36 in) wide fabric; 4 snap fasteners; 1 m ($1\frac{1}{8}$ yd) of ric-rac braid.

To make: Extend lower edge of bodice pattern by 4 cm ($1\frac{1}{2}$ in). Now cut out bodice and sleeve pieces as directed on patterns. Make and finish bodice as for dress bodice. Narrowly hem lower edge and sew snap fasteners to back edges. Sew ric-rac to sleeve and lower edges.

Long-sleeved blouse

You will need: 20 cm ($\frac{1}{4}$ yd) of 91 cm (36 in) wide fabric; elastic.

To make: Extend lower edge of bodice pattern by 4 cm (1½ in) and lower edge of sleeve pattern by 8 cm (3 in). Make and finish as for short-sleeved blouse but hem lower edge of sleeves and thread through elastic to fit doll's wrists. Narrowly hem lower edge of blouse.

Pinafore dress

You will need: 30 cm (⅜ yd) of 91 cm (36 in) wide soft denim fabric; a short length of bias binding; orange thread for contrast stitching; 5 snap fasteners; 2 small buttons.

To make: Cut two skirt pieces as directed on pattern. Cut two pockets, using pattern and adding 1 cm (⅜ in) all round outer edges. Turn in top edges of pockets 1 cm (⅜ in) and stitch close to fold with orange thread, then stitch again 3 mm (⅛ in) away from first line of stitching. Turn in remaining raw edges 5 mm (¼ in) and tack. Stitch pockets to one skirt piece for skirt front.

Join skirt pieces at side edges, leaving 6 cm (2⅜ in) open at top of one seam for side opening. Turn skirt right side out and press seam with opening in it towards front. Neaten raw edges of opening with bias binding. Turn up lower edge of skirt 1 cm (⅜ in) and press, then catch raw edge in place. Stitch hem as for pocket tops.

For waistband cut a strip of fabric 4 by 32 cm (1½ by 12½ in). Bind waist edge of skirt with strip, taking 5 mm (¼ in) seams. Top stitch round edges of waistband. Sew snap fasteners to side opening of skirt.

For bib, cut a piece of fabric 8 by 10 cm (3 by 4 in). Turn in all raw edges 1 cm (⅜ in) and press, except for one long edge. Top stitch bib to match pockets. Slip raw edge of bib inside waistband at centre front and catch in place. For each shoulder strap, cut a strip of fabric 4 by 24 cm (1½ by 9½ in). Turn in all raw edges 5 mm (¼ in) and press, except for one short edge. Fold each strip in half down its length, right side out. Press, then stitch all round close to edges.

Fit skirt on doll with straps over shoulders and crossing over at back. Sew two strap ends inside back of waistband; join other ends to inside top of bib with snap fasteners. Sew buttons to right side of bib.

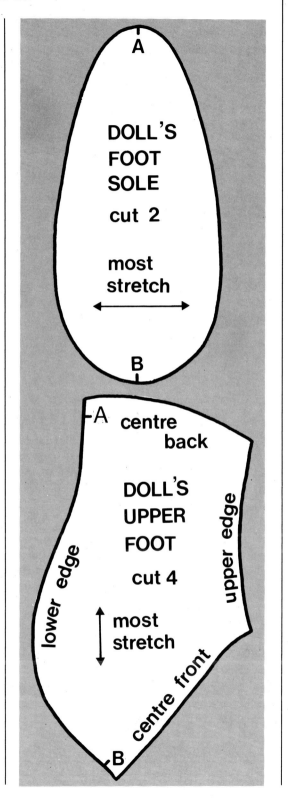

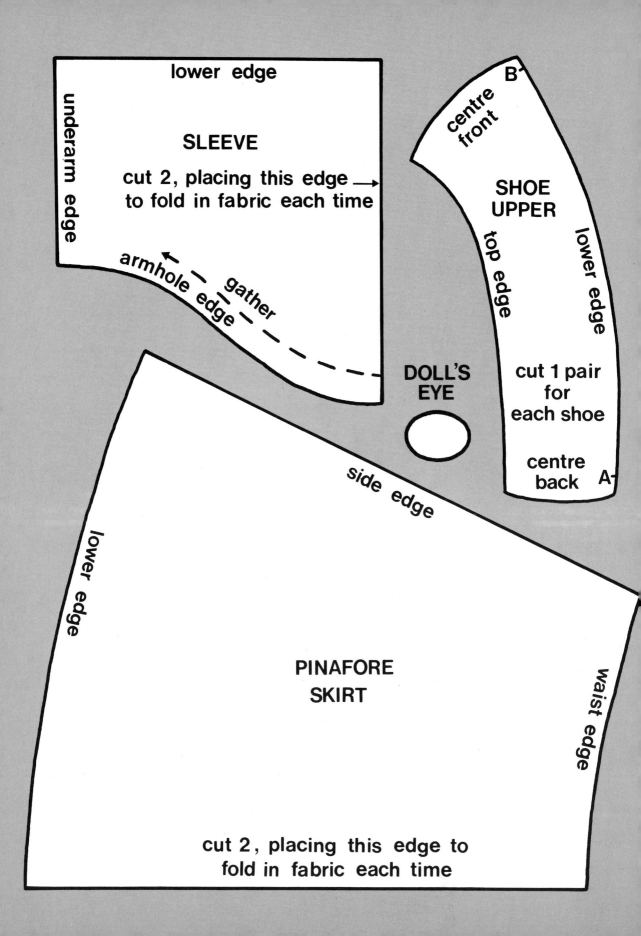

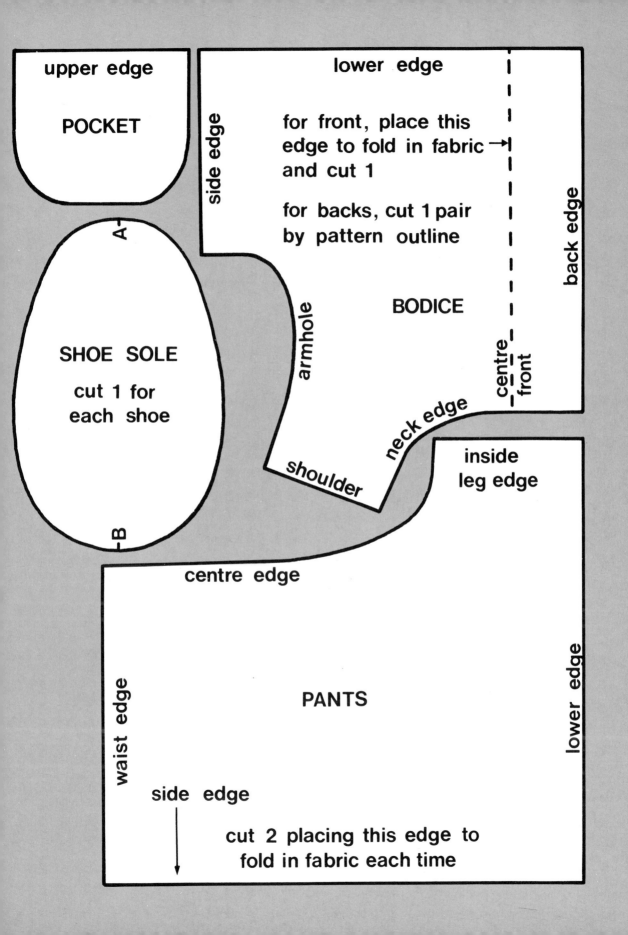

5
ROSETTE DOLLS

Dutch Dolls · 100

*Sam and Sue Scarecrow
103*

Home on the Range · 108

Cowboy · 108
Cowgirl · 109
Horse · 111

Turnabout Dolly · 114

Dutch Dolls

These traditionally dressed Dutch boy and girl are about 36 cm (14 in) tall. They are both rosette dolls and so are very simple to make as their bodies, arms and legs are gathered circles slipped on to elastic

You will need: Oddments of fabrics and felt for gathered circles and clothes; small pieces of stockinette (or cuttings off an old T-shirt) for heads and hands; 2·10 m (2¼ yd) of thin elastic cord; cotton curtain lace and iron-on interlining for girl's bonnet; 25 g of double knitting yarn for hair; stuffing; thin card for circle templates; adhesive; red pencil.

Notes: The seam allowance is 5 mm (¼ in) on stuffed pieces unless otherwise stated.

For fairly authentic costumes, use photographs as a guide to correct colours, noting the following – red and white striped fabric for boy's jacket; multi-coloured striped fabric for girl's skirt, or plain blue instead; flower-patterned fabric for top two circles of girl's bodice.

Make the gathered fabric circles as described on pages 15–16.

Circle diameters

A = 8 cm (3 in)	B = 9 cm (3½ in)
C = 10 cm (4 in)	D = 11 cm (4¼ in)
E = 12 cm (4¾ in)	F = 13 cm (5¼ in)
G = 16 cm (6¼ in)	H = 17 cm (6¾ in)

Dutch boy

Cut out and gather circles as follows: for bodice, six G; for collar, two D; for each sleeve, eight C, six B, and four A; for trouser top five H; for each leg, four F, four E and twelve D.

Head: Cut a 13 by 15 cm (5¼ by 6 in) piece of stockinette with most stretch in the fabric going across the short edge. Join the long edges then gather round one short edge. Pull up gathers tightly and then fasten off. Stuff head firmly and run a gathering thread round remaining raw edge. Cut a 70 cm (27½ in) length of elastic, fold it in half and make a knot in the folded end. Pull up head gathers, turning in raw edges and enclosing knotted end of elastic. Fasten off, oversewing through elastic to secure.

Body and legs: Thread two collar circles on to the double body elastic, then two bodice circles. Cut a 35 cm (13¾ in) length of elastic for the arms and pass it between the body elastics. Thread remaining four bodice circles on to body elastics, then the five trouser top circles.

On to each body elastic, thread leg circles as follows: four F, four E and twelve D. Securely knot each elastic close to last circle, trimming off any excess.

Clogs: Cut four felt clog pieces from pattern. Join them in pairs, stitching close to edges and leaving top edges open. Turn right side out and stuff very firmly. Run gathering threads round top edges and pull up gathers tightly, enclosing knots in leg elastics. Oversew through elastic.

Arms: On to each end of arm elastic, thread sleeve circles as follows: eight C, six B and four A. Knot ends of elastic as for legs. Use the pattern to cut two pairs of hand pieces from stockinette with most stretch in fabric in direction shown on pattern. Join hands in pairs, leaving wrist edges open. Trim seams, turn and stuff, then gather wrist edges and sew to knots as for legs, turning in raw edges of fabric.

Face and hair: Cut eyes from black felt using pattern. Stick them half-way down face and 2·5 cm (1 in) apart. Work a small U-shape for mouth in red thread, 1·5 cm (⅝ in) below eyes. Colour cheeks and nose with red pencil.

For hair, wind yarn four times round two

fingers then slip it off fingers and machine stitch through one end of loops. Continue making loops until a 26 cm (10¼ in) continuous length is formed. Pin and sew this across forehead, round sides and back of head above neck.

Cap: For cap side, cut a 4 by 28 cm (1½ by 11 in) strip of felt. Join short edges then turn in one long edge and stitch down. Run a gathering thread round remaining edge. Cut an 8 cm (3 in) circle of felt for top of cap and oversew it to gathered edge of cap, pulling up gathering thread slightly to ease side of cap to fit top. Turn right side out. Cut two cap peak pieces from felt, placing pattern to fold in felt. Oversew outer edges together then turn right side out. Top-stitch round outer edge. Oversew inner edges of peak to cap front at lower edge. Put a little stuffing inside cap and sew it to head to cover top of hair.

Dutch girl

Cut out and gather fabric circles as for boy, making top two bodice circles from flower patterned fabric. Omit the A sleeve circles.

Head: Make the girl's head exactly in the same way as before.

Skirt and apron: Cut a 20 by 65 cm (8 by 25½ in) strip of fabric. Join short edges and take a narrow hem on one remaining raw edge.

For apron top cut a 7 by 22 cm (2¾ by 8¾ in) strip of striped fabric and a 12 by 22 cm (4¾ by 8¾ in) strip for lower portion. Join them at one long edge. Take a narrow hem round apron except striped edge. Tack this raw edge level with top raw edge of skirt at front. Gather round top raw edge of skirt, pull up gathers until raw edges meet then fasten off.

Body and legs: Make as for boy, threading skirt on to elastics between bodice and pants top circles.

Clogs: Make clogs for the girl in the same way as for boy.

Arms: On to each arm elastic thread arm circles as follows: eight C, and six B circles. Extend wrist edge of hand pattern by 5 cm (2 in) as shown on pattern to form lower portion of arms. Cut out, make and attach as for boy. Tie sewing thread tightly round at position of wrists then sew thread ends into hands. Now sew upper ends of arms to fabric circles where they touch.

Face and hair: Make face as for boy. Cut about forty 50 cm (19½ in) lengths of yarn and tie at centre with a strand of yarn. Sew this centre to forehead 4 cm (1½ in) above eyes. Tie strands again at each side of head, level with mouth, then sew to head. Plait hair. Tie yarn round ends and trim to even lengths.

Lace bonnet: Iron the interlining to wrong side of lace fabric before cutting out pieces from pattern. Cut one pair of bonnet pieces and sew the darts as shown on pattern. Trim darts. Join pieces along top and centre back edges. Make bonnet lining in same way but do not stitch darts. Join bonnet and lining pieces round face and neck edges, leaving a gap in neck edge at back. Turn right side out and slip stitch gap. Stitch all round close to edge of bonnet. Run a gathering thread along neck edge as shown on pattern put bonnet on doll and pull up gathers to fit at back of neck. Fasten off. Stuff top of bonnet then sew to head at each side at position of dotted line shown on pattern.

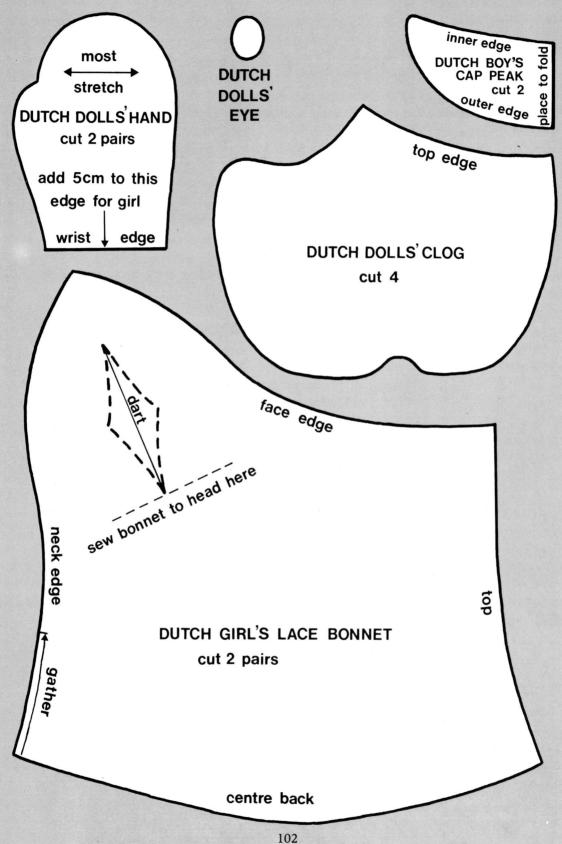

most

stretch

DUTCH DOLLS' HAND

cut 2 pairs

add 5cm to this

edge for girl

wrist ↓ edge

DUTCH DOLLS' EYE

inner edge

DUTCH BOY'S CAP PEAK

cut 2

outer edge

place to fold

top edge

DUTCH DOLLS' CLOG

cut 4

dart

face edge

sew bonnet to head here

neck edge

gather

top

DUTCH GIRL'S LACE BONNET

cut 2 pairs

centre back

Sam and Sue Scarecrow

*Meet Sam and Sue Scarecrow, a pair of 48 cm (19 in) high colourful characters made
from fabric rosettes threaded onto elastic. Smaller rosette circles placed at the knee and
elbow joints enable the dolls to be posed in a variety of amusing ways*

Sam Scarecrow

You will need: Oddments of fabric; for head, pieces cut from discarded nylon stockings or tights; for hair and straw fringe at wrists and ankles, pieces of coarsely woven yellow or orange fabric; for hands, pieces cut from a discarded wool or cotton vest; for boots, small pieces black and brown felt and thin card; small amount stuffing; scraps of blue and black felt for eyes; red and black marker pens; 140 cm (54 in) of thin elastic cord; thin card for circle templates; adhesive.

Notes: Seams as stated in instructions. Make the gathered fabric circles as described on pages 15–16.

Circle diameters

A = 23 cm (9 in)	B = 20 cm (8 in)
C = 15 cm (6 in)	D = 13 cm ($5\frac{1}{4}$ in)
E = 10 cm (4 in)	F = 8 cm (3 in)

Cut out and gather circles as follows.

For each trouser leg, cut twenty C circles, four D circles and four E circles. For top of trousers cut six B circles. For shirt cut eight B circles and for collar three A circles. For each sleeve cut eighteen D circles, four E circles and two F circles.

Straw fringes: For each wrist cut an 8 by 18 cm (3 by 7 in) strip of coarsely woven fabric. Fray out each long edge leaving 2·5 cm (1 in) at centre of strip unfrayed. Join short edges of strip oversewing securely. Fold strip in half down centre and run round a gathering thread about 5 mm ($\frac{1}{4}$ in) from folded edge, pull up gathers tightly and fasten off. For each ankle cut a 10 by 25 cm (4 by 10 in) strip. Make as given for wrist strips.

To assemble the circles: Cut a 71 cm (28 in) length of elastic, fold it in half and push looped end through centres of trouser top circles then through the shirt circles and lastly through the collar circles. Slip a pencil through looped end of elastic to prevent circles slipping off.

Now thread circles for one leg onto one free end of elastic as follows: twelve C, two D, four E, two D, eight C and lastly one ankle

fringe. Knot end of elastic securely and push a darning needle through knot to prevent circles slipping off elastic. Thread remaining leg circles onto other end of elastic in same way.

For the arms cut a 46 cm (18 in) length of elastic and knot one end then push a darning needle through knot to prevent circles from slipping off. Thread circles onto elastic for one sleeve as follows: one wrist fringe, eight D, two E, two F, two E, then ten D circles. Thread unknotted end of arm elastic through the doubled body elastic below the three collar circles. Thread on the remaining sleeve circles for other sleeve working the above sequence in reverse so that eight D circles come at wrist end of arm. Knot end of elastic and push a darning needle through knot.

Head: Cut across leg of nylon stocking or tights close to ankle, then cut leg above ankle into three 15 cm (6 in) long sections. Place these sections inside each other making a triple thickness tube. Run a gathering thread round one end of the tube through all thicknesses 5 mm ($\frac{1}{4}$ in) from edges, pull up gathers tightly and fasten off. Run a loose tacking thread through raw edges at other end of tube to hold the three thicknesses together. Stuff head until it measures about 29 cm ($11\frac{1}{2}$ in) around and 33 cm (13 in) measured from neck edge at front over gathered top of head to neck edge at back; fasten a rubber band round neck end about 4 cm ($1\frac{1}{2}$ in) up from raw edges.

For eyes cut two 1 cm ($\frac{3}{8}$ in) diameter circles of black felt then glue these onto slightly larger ovals of blue felt as shown in illustration. For nose cut a 2·5 cm (1 in) diameter circle from double thickness nylon stocking fabric then run a gathering thread round close to edges. Stuff centre, pull up gathers and fasten off. Sew nose in place about half way down face. Glue eyes in position. Colour cheeks and nose with red pen, smoothing colour into fabric with a paper tissue. Allow to dry, then mark on mouth, eyelashes and eyebrows with black pen. Using black thread work a single line of back stitching along each of these lines.

For hair cut an 18 by 30 cm (7 by 12 in) strip of coarsely woven fabric. Fray out each of the long edges leaving 5 cm (2 in) at centre of strip unfrayed. Join short edges, over-sewing firmly. Fold strip in half down length and run a gathering thread along folded edge. Pull up thread to gather slightly then fasten off. Place gathered edge of hair on top of head having it off centre so that fringe hangs down more at back of head than front. Sew gathered edge to head. (Note that the bare patch on head will be covered by hat later on). Cut hair short above eyes.

Hat: For the hat brim cut two 17 cm (6½ in) diameter circles of fabric and glue them with wrong sides together. Cut a 9 cm (3½ in) diameter circle from centre and discard it then work three rows of machine stitching round brim. Using pattern cut two hat crown pieces placing pattern to fold in fabric each time. Join the pieces with right sides together round curved edges taking 5 mm (¼ in) seam and leaving lower straight edges open. With right sides together, join lower edge of crown to inner edge of brim taking a 3 mm (⅛ in) seam and stitching in a few strands frayed out from the hair fabric as you go, to hang down over brim. Place hat on head and sew to head all round base of crown with long running stitches taking care that stitches do not show on outside of hat.

Run a gathering thread round neck near rubber band, remove band and trim off nylon fabric about 2 cm (¾ in) below gathering thread. Turn in cut edges of neck and place looped elastic end of body into opening. Pull up gathers and oversew neck edges securely at the same time sewing through the elastic.

Hands: Cut out hand pattern from paper and pin this onto double thickness of vest fabric having right sides of fabric together. Stitch round hand close to paper pattern leaving lower straight edges open. Cut out hand close to stitching line. Pull the two layers of fabric apart and stitch a dart across one hand piece only, as shown on pattern. (For second hand, stitch dart on opposite hand piece, to make a pair.) Turn hands right side out and stuff then pin wrist edges of each hand together. Using double brown thread, take stitches around and through hand at thumb and to mark fingers as shown by solid lines on pattern, pull thread fairly tight on each stitch and fasten off by working a tiny oversewing stitch

at base of each finger. Take stab stitches through hand as shown on pattern to hold finger threads in place pulling threads up tight and fastening off as before. Using coloured threads work small darns on hands. Gather raw edges of hands about 1 cm (⅜ in) from edges and sew to knotted ends of arm elastic as for head.

Boots: Cut two soles from brown felt then cut four heel pieces from felt along cutting line indicated on pattern. Glue heel pieces together in pairs then using black thread work a line of running stitches all round 3 mm (⅛ in) from edges. Cut two small patches from black felt and glue one to each felt sole then sew in place with large stitches. For each boot cut two uppers from black felt and stitch them together in pairs at centre front and back edges taking 3 mm (⅛ in) seams. Turn right side out and place uppers in position against soles matching centre front and centre back points. With wrong sides facing join uppers to soles with running stitches using black thread about 3 mm (⅛ in) from edges. Cut two soles from thin card and trim a good 3 mm (⅛ in) off edges. Put card soles inside boots then stuff boots to within 1 cm (⅜ in) of top edges allowing toe ends to turn up, forming creases in the uppers. Glue and sew small patches to uppers then work a few straight stitches across front seams for boot laces. Gather tops of boots 5 mm (¼ in) from edges and sew to knotted ends of leg elastics as for head.

Sue Scarecrow

You will need: Materials as for Sam plus: 1 m (1¼ yd) of broderie Anglaise lace edging about 5 cm (2 in) in width; 23 cm (¼ yd) of 91 cm (36 in) wide fabric for skirt; scraps of orange, yellow and green felt for flowers. Make in the same way as Sam with the following exceptions:

Leg pieces: Use plain white fabric, for example cuttings from an old sheet.

Ankle frills: Cut two 30 cm (12 in) lengths of broderie Anglaise, join short edges taking tiny seams then gather up one long edge of each strip tightly. Thread these onto elastic before fringed circles.

Neck frill: Cut a 38 cm (15 in) length of broderie Anglaise, make as for ankle frills then thread onto loop of elastic after collar circles.

Skirt: Cut a 22 by 82 cm (8½ by 32 in) strip of fabric. Join short edges taking a 1 cm (⅜ in) seam then hem one long edge. For apron cut a 15 cm (6 in) square of fabric, fray out three raw edges and place unfrayed edge of apron even with top raw edge of skirt. Gather up top edge of skirt (including apron) very tightly then fasten off. Place skirt between trouser and shirt circles when assembling. Cut small fabric patches, fray out edges then sew to skirt as illustrated.

Hair: Cut a 30 by 46 cm (12 by 18 in) piece of coarsely woven fabric. Fray out the 30 cm (12 in) edges in same way as for Sam's hair then sew to head. Cut hair short above eyes

then gather remainder of strands to each side of head and plait them. Tie string bows round ends of plaits. Sew tops of plaits to sides of head.

Headscarf: Cut a 30 cm (12 in) square of fabric and fray out edges. Fold into a triangle and place on head joining the three corners of triangle together at back of head. Sew them in this position. Catch scarf to front and sides of head with a few stitches just under folded edge of scarf so that stitches do not show on outside.

Buttercups: Cut a few buttercups from yellow felt then cut 1 cm (⅜ in) diameter circles of orange felt for centres. For each stem cut a 1 by 9 cm (⅜ by 3½ in) strip of green felt. Oversew long edges of each strip. Pierce a hole in centre of each buttercup then push one end of stem through and sew in place. Glue orange centres to flowers to cover ends of stems. Cut small piece of green felt for leaf and sew to stem. Sew bunch of buttercups to hand.

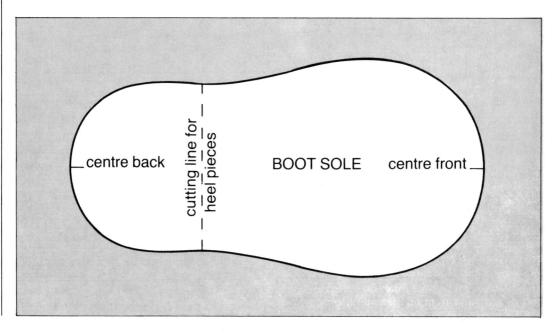

centre back ¦ cutting line for heel pieces ¦ BOOT SOLE ¦ centre front

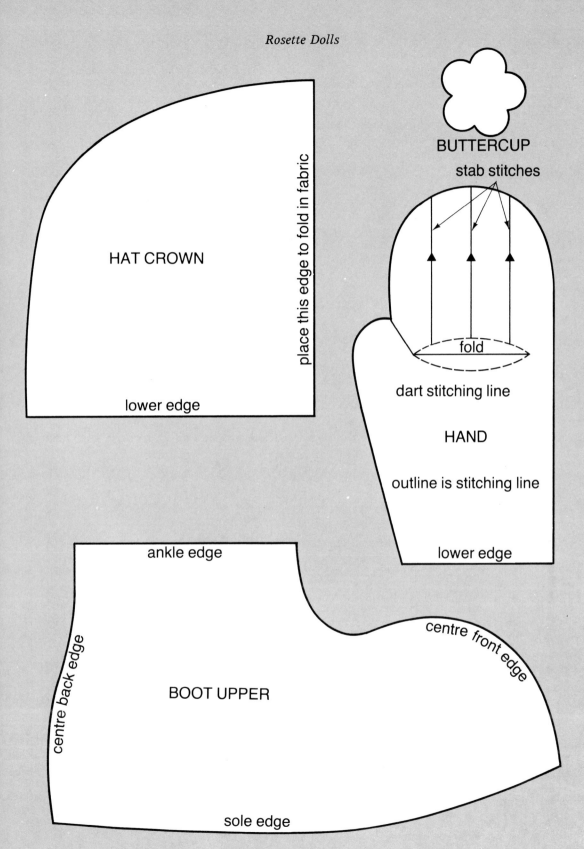

HAT CROWN

place this edge to fold in fabric

lower edge

BUTTERCUP

stab stitches

fold

dart stitching line

HAND

outline is stitching line

lower edge

ankle edge

centre front edge

centre back edge

BOOT UPPER

sole edge

Home on the Range

Three colourful characters from the Wild West – a cheery cowboy, his pretty partner and, of course, his horse. They are all stretchy toys made of gathered circles of fabric threaded on elastic. The finished dolls are about 55 cm (21½ in) high and the horse is about 27 cm (10¾ in) tall

The cowboy

You will need: Oddments of fabric; for head and hands – a pair of stretchy nylon tights or stockings (one leg makes one doll); for hair – a small ball of thick-knit yarn and 34 cm (13½ in) of tape or bias binding; felt for hat, waist-coat and shoe soles; a little stuffing; 60 cm (23½ in) of narrow braid for trimming boots; thin card for circle templates; 120 cm (47¼ in) of thin elastic cord; black felt, red pencil, black and white thread for features; adhesive.

Notes: Seams as stated in instructions. Make the gathered fabric circles as described on pages 15–16.

Circle diameters
A = 20 cm (8 in)	B = 18 cm (7 in)
C = 14 cm (5½ in)	D = 12 cm (4¾ in)
E = 10 cm (4 in)	F = 8 cm (3 in)

Cut out and gather circles as follows.

For each trouser leg cut twenty C circles, four D and two E circles.

For top of trousers cut four A circles. For belt cut two A circles. For shirt cut six A circles. For top of shirt cut three B circles. For collar cut two C circles.

For each sleeve cut sixteen D circles, four E circles and two F circles.

To assemble the circles: Cut a 76 cm (30 in) length of elastic, fold it in half and push looped end through centres of trouser top circles, then through the belt, shirt, shirt top and lastly collar circles. Knot looped end of elastic and push a needle through knot to stop circles slipping off.

Now thread circles for one leg on to one free end of elastic as follows – ten C circles,

two D, two E, two D, and lastly ten C circles. Make a large knot in end of elastic and push a needle through as before. Thread on other leg circles in same way.

For arms cut a 44 cm (17½ in) length of elastic. Make a large knot in one end and push a needle through knot. Thread circles on to elastic for one sleeve as follows – eight D circles, two E, two F, two E, and lastly eight D circles. Thread unknotted end of elastic through doubled body elastic below the five shirt top and collar circles. Thread on remaining circles for other sleeve as for first sleeve. Knot end of elastic and push a needle through to hold circles.

Head: Cut across one leg of tights or stockings close to ankle, then cut leg above ankle into three sections 12 cm (4¾ in) long. Place these inside each other to make a triple-thickness tube, with raw edges level. Run a gathering thread round 1 cm (⅜ in) from one end of tube through all thicknesses, pull up gathers tightly and fasten off. Turn tube right side out, tack the three layers together at raw edges. Stuff head to measure about 33 cm (13 in) around, and 30 cm (12 in) measuring from neck edge at front, over gathered top of head to neck edge at back. Fasten a rubber band round neck end, about 4 cm (1½ in) up from raw edges.

For eyes cut two 1·5 cm (⅝ in) diameter circles of black felt. Using white thread work a few small straight stitches on each eye as shown in our picture. Glue eyes to head half-way down face, 3·5 cm (1⅜ in) apart. Colour cheeks with moistened red pencil.

Work eyelashes and nose with straight stitches. Work mouth in back stitch, then oversew, working back through each stitch.

For hair cut yarn into 8 cm (3 in) lengths and stitch centre of lengths down centre of tape or binding until it is covered. Fold yarn strands in half round tape (folding tape along its length) and stitch through looped ends of yarn and folded tape, to form a fringe. Over-sew top of fringe to head above eyes and round back of head.

For hat brim cut a 22 cm (8¾ in) diameter circle of felt with a 10 cm (4 in) diameter circle cut out of centre.

For hat crown cut two felt pieces 16 by 12 cm (6¼ by 4¾ in). Join crown pieces round edges taking 5 mm (¼ in) seam, leaving one pair of long edges open and rounding off other corners for top of hat. Trim seam and press. Turn crown right side out and sew lower edge of crown to inner edge of brim, taking a tiny seam.

Put a little stuffing in crown to shape it and make a dent in crown centre. Place hat on head, with lower edge of crown resting on top of hair. Sew hat to head through lower edge of crown. Catch brim to crown at centre front and back.

Run a gathering thread round neck near rubber band, remove band and trim off nylon fabric about 1 cm (⅜ in) below gathering thread. Turn in cut edges of neck and place knotted end of body elastic into opening. Pull up gathers and oversew neck edges securely, sewing through elastic.

Hands: For each hand pin pattern on to three layers of nylon fabric folded in half, with edge of pattern marked fold against fold in fabric. Stitch round hand close to pattern, leaving lower straight edges open. Cut out hand close to stitching. Turn right side out and stuff. Make thumb by taking a large stitch round hand at one side, pulling stitch up tight.

Gather round raw edges of hands 1 cm (⅜ in) from edges and sew to knotted ends of arm elastic as for head.

Boots: Cut two soles from card. Cut two pairs of uppers from fabric and join them in pairs at centre front and back edges, taking narrow seams. Turn right side out and place a card sole inside lower edge of each boot, matching centre front and back points. Glue lower edges of uppers 5 mm (¼ in) on to card soles.

Cut two felt soles and glue them in place to cover card soles and raw fabric edges. Stuff

boots to within 2 cm (¾ in) of top edges. Glue braid round boots at lower edges. Gather boot tops and sew to knotted ends of leg elastic as for head.

Waistcoat: Cut two fronts and one back from felt, as directed on pattern. Join fronts to back at sides, oversewing edges together. Fold back lapels on fronts and press.

Machine round edges of waistcoat and lapels. Join shoulder seams, oversewing edges together. Press seams.

Neckerchief: Cut a triangle of fabric, 50 cm (19½ in) across the base by 20 cm (8 in) high. Hem edges and knot round doll's neck.

The cowgirl

You will need: Materials as for boy (omitting tape for hair, braid, felt for hat and waistcoat). Also 3 m (3⅜ yd) lace edging, 4 cm (1½ in) wide; quilted fabric for bonnet; 30 by 91 cm (11¾ by 36 in) of printed fabric for skirt; same amount of plain fabric for underskirt; 1·5 m (1⅝ yd) of ribbon for trimming bonnet and shoes; 10 cm (4 in) of narrow elastic.

To make circles: Work as for Cowboy, but make the two belt circles from same fabric as used for legs.

The lace frills: For each cuff frill cut a 30 cm (12 in) length of lace edging. Join short edges, gather up one long edge tightly and fasten off. For neck frill cut a 40 cm (15¾ in) length, make in same way.

The skirt: Join short edges of fabric. Make a 4 cm (1½ in) hem on one long raw edge, then sew on lace edging. Gather round other remaining raw edge tightly, fasten off.

The underskirt: Make as for skirt, taking a slightly larger hem and sewing on lace edging so it hangs slightly below skirt hem.

To assemble the circles: Work as for Cowboy, threading on lace frills at neck and wrist edges. Thread underskirt and skirt on to elastic between top of belt and shirt circles.

The head: Make as for Cowboy except for hair. Wind yarn into a hank measuring about 50 cm (19½ in). Back stitch strands of yarn at centre of hank to centre top of head. Take yarn loops to each side of head and sew in place in a bunch. Cut through yarn loops to separate strands, then trim ends evenly.

For bonnet brim cut two fabric strips 27 by 7 cm (10⅝ by 2¾ in). Join edges taking a 5 mm (¼ in) seam, leaving one pair of long edges open and rounding off other corners. Trim seam and turn right side out. Top stitch through brim close to seam edge, then tack raw edges together.

For back of bonnet cut a 40 cm (15¾ in) diameter semi-circle. Turn in straight edge

110

1 cm ($\frac{3}{8}$ in) and hem. Thread narrow elastic through hem, securing elastic each end with a few stitches. Gather curved edge of semi-circle to fit raw edges of brim; join them taking a 5 mm ($\frac{1}{4}$ in) seam.

Decorate bonnet by sewing a strip of ribbon across brim, and a ribbon rosette to each side. Place bonnet on head behind hair and catch it to head with stitches at each side, lower back edge and top of brim. Sew head to elastic as for Cowboy.

The hands: Make as for Cowboy.

The boots: Make and sew to leg elastics as before, cutting upper edges of boot uppers along dotted line shown on pattern. Omit braid, and sew a ribbon bow to front of each boot.

The horse

You will need: Oddments of fabric; for head, ears and hooves – a pair of men's plain socks (such as stretchy towelling ones); a small ball of thick-knit yarn for mane and tail; a little stuffing; thin card for soles of hooves and for circle templates; 170 cm (67 in) of thin elastic cord; scraps of felt for soles of hooves, eyes and nostrils; thin yarn for mouth; 1 m (39$\frac{1}{2}$ in) of braid for reins; adhesive.

Circle diameters
A = 24 cm (9$\frac{1}{2}$ in)   B = 22 cm (8$\frac{3}{4}$ in)
C = 20 cm (8 in)   D = 18 cm (7 in)
E = 16 cm (6$\frac{1}{4}$ in)   F = 14 cm (5$\frac{1}{2}$ in)
G = 12 cm (4$\frac{3}{4}$ in)   H = 10 cm (4 in)
I = 8 cm (3 in)

Cut out and gather circles as follows.

For neck cut fourteen E size circles and two D circles.

For body cut two D circles, four C, four B, and six A circles.

For rear end of body cut two B circles, one D, one E, one F and one G circle.

For each front leg cut two E circles, twelve F, ten G, four H and two I circles.

For each back leg cut two D circles, two E, ten F, ten G, four H and two I circles.

To assemble the circles: Cut two 45 cm (17$\frac{3}{4}$ in) lengths of elastic for legs and put them aside.

For body cut 80 cm (31$\frac{1}{2}$ in) of elastic, fold it in half and knot ends together, slipping a needle through knot. Push opposite looped end of elastic through body circles as follows (starting at rear of body) – one G, one F, one E, one D, two B circles. Now thread one length of leg elastic through the doubled body elastic.

Continue threading on body circles – six A, four B, four C, two D circles. Now thread remaining length of leg elastic through the doubled body elastic.

Thread on neck circles – two D and fourteen E circles. Knot looped end of elastic and push a needle through knot.

Thread front leg circles for each leg on to each appropriate end of elastic as follows – two E, twelve F, two G, two H, two I, two H, and eight G circles. Knot elastic ends and push needles through knots.

Thread back leg circles on to each end of leg elastic as follows – two D, two E, ten F, two G, two H, two I, two H, and eight G circles. Knot elastic ends and push needles through knots to hold circles.

Head: Stuff the foot of one sock into a slightly tapered shape, about 20 cm (8 in) long by about 28 cm (11 in) around widest part. Cut off sock foot at an angle (see diagram 1), for neck edge of head. Gather round this cut edge about 1 cm ($\frac{3}{8}$ in) from edge. Turn in raw edge and pull up gathering thread, pushing knotted neck end of body elastic inside head. Pull up gathers and oversew securely through elastic to hold it in place.

From blue felt cut two oval shapes from eye pattern. Cut two circles of black felt, and glue them to blue pieces as shown on pattern. Work a few small straight stitches in white thread at top of each eye, as shown in illustration. Glue eyes to head.

Cut two 2 cm ($\frac{3}{4}$ in) diameter circles of pink felt for nostrils and two slightly smaller black felt circles. Glue black circles to centres of pink ones, then glue nostrils in place.

Using doubled thin yarn, work mouth round end of face, taking a large stitch round from one side to the other.

Make a triangular pattern for ears, 8 cm

(3 in) across the base by 9 cm ($3\frac{1}{2}$ in) high. Cut two ear pieces from remaining piece of sock, and also two from fabric. Join pieces in pairs, taking 5 mm ($\frac{1}{4}$ in) seam, leaving base edges open and rounding off points at tops. Trim off points and turn ears right side out. Turn in remaining raw edges 5 mm ($\frac{1}{4}$ in) and oversew pulling stitches to gather slightly. Fold ears and sew folded lower edges to head.

Mane: Cut about twenty 30 cm (12 in) lengths of yarn. Fold them in half and tie a yarn strand round, about 7·5 cm (3 in) from folded ends. Sew this tied point to top of head just behind ears, so looped ends hang over forehead.

Tail: Cut yarn lengths as for mane. Thread lengths through knotted elastic at end of body, and fold in half to hang down evenly. Tie a yarn strand round close to folded ends, enclosing elastic knot.

Hooves: Cut four 7 cm ($2\frac{3}{4}$ in) diameter circles of card. From the remaining sock cut four tubular sections, each 6 cm ($2\frac{3}{8}$ in) long, cutting right across leg and foot of sock as shown in diagram 2. Place a card circle 1 cm ($\frac{3}{8}$ in) inside one raw edge of each tube, and stick fabric edges on to card.

Stuff each hoof and gather all round close to remaining raw edge. Turn in raw edge, pull up gathers and enclose knotted end of leg elastic, oversewing securely through elastic to hold knot in place.

Glue a 7 cm ($2\frac{3}{4}$ in) diameter circle of felt to sole of each hoof to cover raw edges.

Reins: Cut a 25 cm ($9\frac{3}{4}$ in) length of braid, overlap short ends 1 cm ($\frac{3}{8}$ in) and sew in place. Slip this circle over horse's nose and pin ends of remaining braid to it each side. Take reins off horse and sew ends of braid in place.

For rosettes make two 8 cm (3 in) diameter gathered circles, turning in edges when gathering. Sew one each side of reins to complete the horse.

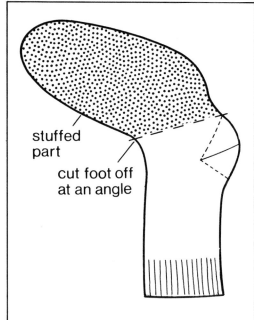

stuffed part

cut foot off at an angle

Diagram 1 How to make horse's head

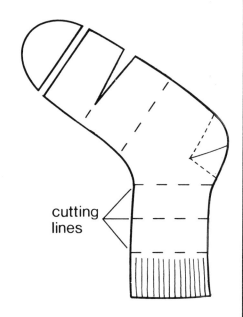

cutting lines

Diagram 2 Cutting the 6 cm ($2\frac{3}{8}$ in) sections for horse's hooves

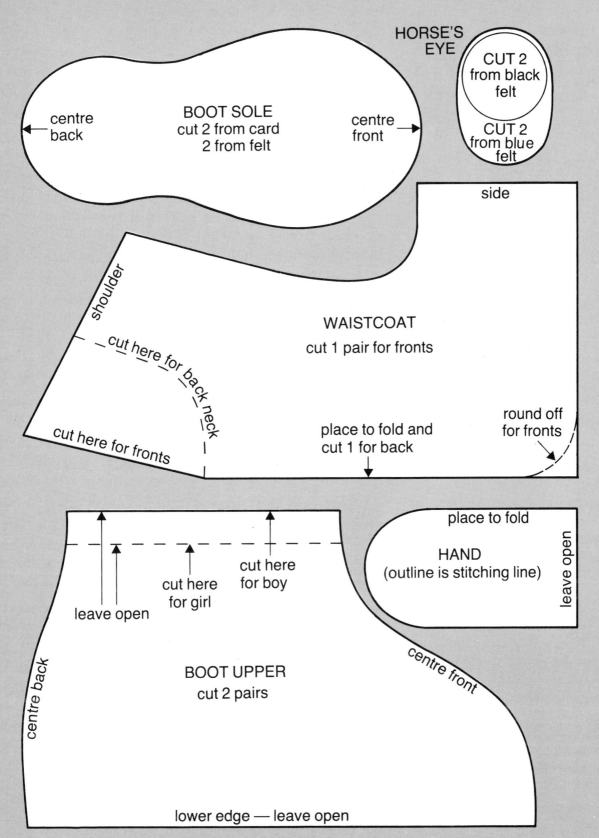

HORSE'S EYE

CUT 2 from black felt

CUT 2 from blue felt

BOOT SOLE
cut 2 from card
2 from felt

centre back

centre front

side

WAISTCOAT
cut 1 pair for fronts

shoulder

cut here for back neck

cut here for fronts

place to fold and cut 1 for back

round off for fronts

place to fold

HAND
(outline is stitching line)

leave open

leave open

cut here for girl

cut here for boy

centre back

BOOT UPPER
cut 2 pairs

centre front

lower edge — leave open

Turnabout Dolly

This 43 cm (17 in) double-ended doll has a dual personality. At one end she's a smiling brunette; turn her upside down and she's a beautiful blonde with a tearful face. Easy and inexpensive to make from gathered fabric circles with a pair of socks used for the heads and hands.

You will need: One pair of size 9 ankle socks (preferably with a plain-knit sole) in pink or white; about half a ball each of black and yellow 4-ply knitting yarn; scraps of black and blue felt; 2·5 m (2¾ yd) of 4 cm (1½ in) wide broderie Anglaise edging; stuffing; 1 m (1 yd) of thin elastic cord; adhesive; red pencil.

For each doll's dress; 1·2 m (1¼ yd) of 91 cm (36 in) wide gingham; scraps of contrast coloured fabric for collar and cuffs; 2 m (2 yd) ric-rac braid to match contrasting fabrics; scraps of ribbon; thin card for circle templates.

Notes: Seams as stated in instructions. Make the gathered fabric circles as described on pages 15–16. Before cutting out the gingham circles, first cut a 30 by 91 cm (12 by 36 in) strip from each piece of gingham for each doll's skirt.

Circle diameters

A = 18 cm (7 in)   B = 15 cm (6 in)
C = 10 cm (4 in)

Cut out and gather circles as follows.

For each doll's bodice, cut five A circles from gingham, then cut two B circles from contrast fabric for each doll's collar. For each sleeve cut seventeen C circles from gingham then cut one C circle from contrast fabric.

Broderie Anglaise frills: For frills at neck and wrists of both dolls cut six 25 cm (10 in) lengths of broderie Anglaise. Join short edges of each strip taking tiny seams then run a gathering thread along raw edge, pull up gathers tightly and fasten off. (Trim a little off long raw edges of four of the strips before gathering up, to make narrower frills for the wrists.)

Skirt: Stitch two rows of ric-rac braid near one long edge of each gingham strip spaced as shown in the illustrations, this will be the hem edge. With right sides facing, join short edges of each skirt strip taking a 1 cm (⅜ in) seam. With raw edges level sew broderie Anglaise trimming to hem edge of one skirt piece on right side. Having right sides together join both skirt pieces at hem edges taking a 1 cm (⅜ in) seam. Turn right side out bringing raw edges together then press. Using strong thread, run a gathering thread round

1 cm (⅜ in) from raw edges through both thicknesses of fabric. Pull up gathers tightly and fasten off.

To assemble the body pieces: Cut a 25 cm (10 in) length of elastic, fold it in half and knot ends together. Push looped end of elastic through circles and other pieces as follows: thread on one broderie Anglaise collar frill, two B contrast colour collar circles, five A gingham bodice circles, then the skirt (taking care to have correct fabric against matching bodice circles), remaining five A gingham bodice circles, two other B contrast colour collar circles and lastly one broderie Anglaise collar frill. Slip a pencil through knotted and looped ends of elastic to prevent circles slipping off.

To assemble the arm pieces: Cut a 33 cm (13 in) length of elastic and knot one end then push a darning needle through knot to prevent circles slipping off. Thread on one broderie Anglaise wrist frill, one C contrast colour circle, then seventeen sleeve circles. Thread the un-knotted end of the elastic through doubled body elastic below top four collar and bodice circles at one end of body. Now thread on the remaining sleeve circles and lastly the C contrast colour circle and the broderie Anglaise frill. Knot end of elastic and push a darning needle through knot.

Make up the other pair of arms in the same way threading elastic through doubled body elastic at other end of doll.

Head with crying face: Stuff the toe of one sock firmly to form a ball about 28 cm (11 in) in circumference. Secure sock at neck end with a rubber band and use plainest part of sock for face. For eyes cut two 1·5 cm (½ in) diameter circles of blue felt and two of black felt. Trim a little off one side of each black circle and glue to blue circles as shown in illustration. Glue eyes to head about 6·5 cm (2½ in) up from rubber band having them about 2·5 cm (1 in) apart. Work straight stitches for eyelashes using black thread. Colour cheeks with moistened red pencil then work tears in single large chain stitches using black thread. Using white thread work a few tiny satin stitches at base of each tear for a highlight. Work nose and mouth with red thread as illustrated. For hair, wind most of the yellow yarn into a hank 20 cm (8 in) long. Tie a length of matching yarn round centre of hank. Place this tied centre at top of head so that looped ends will hang down further at back of head than front. Sew tied centre of yarn in position. Spread out loops evenly all round head and sew ends of loops to head as illustrated taking care to make stitches as small as possible. Make a small bunch of yarn from remainder and twist and sew it to top of head for a top knot of hair. Sew small ribbon bow to front of top knot.

Run a gathering thread round neck near rubber band, remove band, pull up gathers then cut off remainder of sock 1 cm ($\frac{3}{8}$ in) below thread. Turn in cut edges of neck and place looped or knotted end of body elastic into neck opening. Pull up gathers and over-sew edges firmly, enclosing elastic in stitching.

Head with smiling face: Stuff head and make eyes, eyelashes and nose as for other head. Work smiling mouth as illustrated. For hair, make a 25 cm (10 in) hank of yarn using most of the yarn. Tie hank at centre and sew to top of head as given for other head. Divide looped ends to either side of face. Sew ends of loops evenly in place all round head as for other head then back stitch through yarn strands all round head about 2·5 cm (1 in) up from looped ends. Sew a few short loops of yarn to forehead above face for a fringe then sew ribbon bow above fringe. Attach head to other end of body elastic in same way as given for other head.

Hands: Using remaining pieces of socks, cut out four hand pieces using pattern and placing edge indicated against a fold for each one. Stitch a narrow seam on each hand as shown on pattern leaving straight edges open. Turn hands right side out and stuff. Gather open raw edges of each hand 1 cm ($\frac{3}{8}$ in) from edge, turn in raw edges and place knotted end of arm elastic inside each opening. Pull up gathers and oversew, enclosing elastic in stitching.

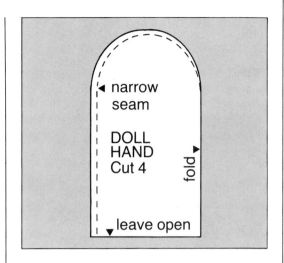

narrow seam

DOLL HAND Cut 4

fold

leave open

6
NOVELTY TOYS

Puppets for a Pantomime
120
Dancing Clown · 124
Bedtime Favourites · 130
Funny Bunny · 134

Puppets for a Pantomime

Aladdin is one of the most popular traditional pantomines and here instructions are given for making the main characters – Aladdin, Widow Twankey, the Princess, wicked Abanazer and two genies of the lamp. The puppets are about 48 cm (19 in) tall and are held by rods hidden under clothing. Each main character has an additional rod attached to one hand which allows it to gesticulate and appear more life-like. Even the smallest child can hold and play with these puppets easily

For each puppet you will need: Small pieces of pink or white cotton stockinette fabric (such as a vest or T-shirt fabric); cotton wool, stuffing, a wire coathanger; one 45 cm (18 in) bamboo garden cane for each puppet except genies; oddments of fabrics; felt; thin fabric for genies; sequins; braid; trimmings; card; yarn for hair; coloured pencils; felt and threads for facial features; scrap of Velcro fastener for positioning Aladdin's un-wired hand; bits of junk jewellery; two curtain rings; one stud-type pierced earring for the magic ring; short lengths of cotton tape about 1·5 cm ($\frac{5}{8}$ in) wide; adhesive.

Notes: The seam allowance is 5 mm ($\frac{1}{4}$ in) on all basic puppet pieces and 1 cm ($\frac{3}{8}$ in) on garment pieces unless otherwise stated.

Cut out stockinette pieces with most stretch in fabric going across the measurement stated in instructions.

Copy pattern outlines square by square on to 5 cm squared graph paper.

Aladdin

Take the bamboo cane for centre rod of puppet and wrap cotton wool round the narrow end, securing with tape.

For head cut a piece of stockinette 13 by 16 cm (5 by $6\frac{1}{4}$ in) with most stretch across the shorter measurement. Join the long edges. Gather round one remaining raw edge, pull up tightly and fasten off. Turn right side out and stuff top. Push padded end of rod inside head and stuff, working round the rod until head measures about 24 cm ($9\frac{1}{2}$ in) round. Run a gathering thread round, 2 cm ($\frac{3}{4}$ in) from remaining raw edge, pull up tightly and fasten off. Stick the raw edges to rod, then

glue tape around them, sticking the tape to rod also.

For body cut a piece of stockinette 12 by 18 cm ($4\frac{3}{4}$ by 7 in) with most stretch across the short measurement. Join long edges and turn right side out. Turn in one remaining raw edge and run a gathering thread round. Slip body onto rod and pull up gathers below head. Fasten off, then sew gathers to head. Stuff body to measure about 18 cm (7 in) round, keeping rod at centre. Gather and secure lower edge of body to rod as for head.

Cut two pairs of hand pieces from stockinette. Join one pair leaving wrist edges open. Join other pair as far as point A and leaving wrist edges open (the wire rod will be inserted in this hand). Trim seams and turn hands right side out.

Cut coathanger as shown in diagram 1, bend round one end to fit inside hand and straighten other end as shown in diagram. For the handle, bend round 8 cm (3 in) at straight end of wire as shown in diagram 2, then bind this end with tape, glueing it in place. At hand end of wire, pad round wire with cotton wool, sewing it in place, then slip wire inside hand and stuff hand to shape. Gather round wrist edge and fasten off, then slip stitch gap from wrist to point A. Stuff remaining hand to size of other hand and gather wrist.

For each sleeve cut a piece of fabric suitable for the puppet's undersleeves 10 by 16 cm (4 by $6\frac{1}{4}$ in). Join long edges and turn right side out. Turn in one raw edge and slip it over gathered end of each hand. Slip stitch in place and stick on trimming. Stuff lower portion of sleeves then run a gathering thread across sleeves 6 cm ($2\frac{3}{8}$ in) from wrist edges. Pull up gathers and fasten off. Put a little stuffing in tops of sleeves, gather up raw edges tightly and sew one to each side of body

120

1 cm ($\frac{3}{8}$ in) down from neck, taking care to have thumbs pointing inwards to body.

Tunic: Cut two tunic pieces placing edge indicated on pattern to fold in fabric each time. Join pieces at shoulders from wrist edges to points A. Hem wrist edges taking 1 cm ($\frac{3}{8}$ in) turnings twice then sew on trimming. Join side and underarm edges and clip seams as shown. Turn right side out and hem lower edge. Slip tunic on puppet pulling wired hand through one sleeve, and the rod through neck opening. Bring shoulder edges together turning in raw edges, then slip stitch as far as neck keeping neck at centre. Sew to neck. Pin braid round neck then take to right-hand side seam of tunic as shown in illustration. Sew braid in place as pinned.

Face and hair: Cut eyes from black felt and stick in place halfway down face and 2·5 cm (1 in) apart. Cut a 2 cm ($\frac{3}{4}$ in) diameter circle of stockinette, gather round edge and stuff, for nose. Sew to face then work mouth and eye lines in thread. Colour cheeks and nose with red pencil.

Cut about thirty 70 cm ($27\frac{1}{2}$ in) lengths of black yarn. Back stitch centres to position of centre parting. Take strands to each side of head and sew there as for centre parting. Plait strands at back of head.

Hat: Cut hat from thin card. Stick fabric to one side of card then form into a cone-shape by overlapping and glueing straight edges as shown on pattern, with fabric on inside of

cone. Cut another piece of fabric slightly larger all round than hat pattern. Place right side out over outside of hat and pin straight edges together to fit. Seam as pinned, turn right side out and place over hat. Stick edges to hat all round, trimming off any excess fabric. Glue braid round edge of hat then stick hat to head.

Magic ring: Fix pierced earring through unwired hand when required. Sew small piece of hooked Velcro to this hand and furry piece of Velcro to tunic at front so that hand may be fixed in place and ring may be rubbed with other hand.

Magic lamp: Cut two from felt and oversew them together leaving lower edges open. Turn and stuff then oversew lower edges. Glue and sew braid round lamp as illustrated, leaving a loop of braid for handle large enough to fit round puppet's unwired hand. Add other ornamentation as available.

The princess

Make basic puppet and tunic as for Aladdin and trim tunic as illustrated. Make basic hair as for Aladdin sewing it to sides of head. Twist strands of yarn and take each to centre top of head then sew there. Take remainder of strands down back of head and tuck ends under then sew in place above neck. If necessary cover remainder of back of head with yarn strands in the same way. Cut eyes from black felt, eyelids from pink felt, then glue them in place and work eye, mouth and nose stitches as illustrated. Sew on beads for earrings, or use other scraps of jewellery.

Head-dress: Cut two from thin card. Cover each with fabric, turning raw edges of fabric to other side of card and glueing down. Stick wrong sides of card pieces together. Glue trimming round edge and jewel to front. For veil, cut a 30 cm (12 in) square of thin fabric and join two opposite edges. Place this seam at centre then join remaining raw edges leaving a gap in one seam. Turn right side out and slip stitch gap. Gather one short edge of veil to 4 cm ($1\frac{1}{2}$ in) and sew it to inner edge of

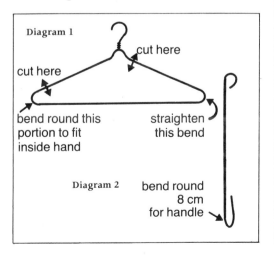

Diagram 1

cut here

cut here

bend round this
portion to fit
inside hand

straighten
this bend

Diagram 2

bend round
8 cm
for handle

head-dress. Sew trimming to other edge of veil. Place head-dress on head behind twists of hair then sew it to each side of head.

Widow Twankey

Make basic puppet as for Aladdin using stockinette pieces 15 by 16 cm (6 by $6\frac{1}{4}$ in) for head and 14 by 18 cm ($5\frac{1}{2}$ by 7 in) for body. Make arms but do not sew them to body at this stage. Make hair as for Aladdin, sewing to sides of head, then curl up the strands to form a sausage curl at each side. Sew curls to head. Sew on beads or other junk jewellery for earrings. Make nose as for Aladdin. Cut eyes from blue felt, add smaller ovals of black felt and stick them above nose. Work other facial lines in thread as illustrated.

Dress: Cut a piece of fabric 40 by 60 cm (16 by $23\frac{1}{2}$ in) then join short edges. Turn right side out and hem one remaining raw edge. Turn in and gather other raw edge round neck then sew to neck. Sew frill of trimming round neck. Run a gathering thread round dress 30 cm (12 in) from hem edge, pull up to body and fasten off. Now sew arms in place through dress at each side of body. For puffed sleeves cut two pieces of fabric 15 by 22 cm (6 by $8\frac{3}{4}$ in). Join short edges and turn right side out. Turn in one remaining raw edge and gather, then place round top of arm. Pull up gathers and sew to dress round arm. Turn in and gather remaining raw edge below elbow and sew to arm. Glue trimming round at this position.

Apron: Cut a piece of fabric 20 by 26 cm (8 by $10\frac{1}{4}$ in). Narrowly hem and sew trimming to all but one short edge. Gather this edge and sew to front waist. Cut a strip of fabric 6 by 50 cm ($2\frac{3}{8}$ by $19\frac{1}{2}$ in) and fold in half along the length. Join long edges and across one short edge. Turn right side out and neaten short raw edge. Sew centre of strip to front waist of apron then tie ends at back.

Hat: Cut a piece of fabric 30 by 60 cm (12 by $23\frac{1}{2}$ in). Join the short edges. Fold up one raw edge to meet the other, with right side of fabric outside. Gather raw edges tightly and

fasten off then turn hat right side out. Gather round hat 5 cm (2 in) from fold, pull up gathers to fit behind hair then fasten off. Stuff top of hat, sew to head through gathers then sew bow to front.

Abanazar

Make basic puppet as for Aladdin, using a piece of fabric 11 by 18 cm ($4\frac{1}{4}$ by 7 in) for the head. Sew a triangle of contrast-coloured fabric to front of tunic as shown by dotted line on tunic pattern. Use a 3 cm ($1\frac{1}{4}$ in) diameter circle of stockinette for nose, stuffing it into a sausage-shape. Use smaller ovals of black felt for eyes and short thin strips of black felt for eyebrows. Work other facial lines as illustrated. Cut two beard and two moustache pieces from felt. Oversew pieces together all round edges, pushing in a little stuffing before completing sewing. Sew to face as illustrated and catch moustache to beard where they touch.

Fez: Cut a 26 cm ($10\frac{1}{4}$ in) diameter semi-circle of thin card. Form into a cone measuring 7 cm ($2\frac{3}{4}$ in) across base. Cover as for Aladdin's hat then stick fez to back of head.

Turban: Use a piece of thin fabric about 25 by 80 cm ($9\frac{3}{4}$ by $31\frac{1}{2}$ in). Gather one end and sew to centre front at base of fez. Wind turban around head, catching in place with stitches and ending with a tail of fabric at one side. Sew on a feather and pin a brooch or sew a button to front of turban. Sew on curtain rings for earrings.

Scarf: Cut a piece of fabric 8 by 20 cm (3 by 8 in). Hem all edges and sew fringe to ends. Fold and drape round shoulders as illustrated and catch to puppet with a few stitches.

The genies

Use a different coloured thin fabric for each one. Use a coathanger, snipping off the top hooked portion only. Straighten out the bends, then bend round the ends of wire as for the wired hand on the other puppets and bind the handle with tape. Bend remainder of wire into an S-shape. Make head as for Aladdin, using a piece of stockinette 15 by 18 cm (6 by 7 in). Stuff head and insert padded end of wire as for bamboo rod. Cut strips of thin fabric and wind around wire to cover it, sewing it to head and handle at each end. For the 'curl of smoke' effect on the wire, cut 20 cm (8 in) wide pieces of fabric to make a 2 m ($2\frac{1}{4}$ yd) length. Join long edges of strip, tapering seam towards one end. Trim seam and turn right side out. Slip this fabric tube over wire and sew wide end to head. Twist and pucker the fabric to fit over the wire as

illustrated, then sew narrow end to handle.

Make nose as for Abanazar, using the thin fabric. Cut largest eye shapes from coloured felt, smaller shapes from black felt. Stick a sequin to centre of each then glue eyes in place. Stick row of sequins above eyes. Make beard and moustache from felt as for Abanazar, but using genie patterns. Before sewing these in place glue a small piece of black felt below nose.

Make turban as for Abanazar but using a little more fabric if necessary and starting by taking fabric from front to back of head to cover the top.

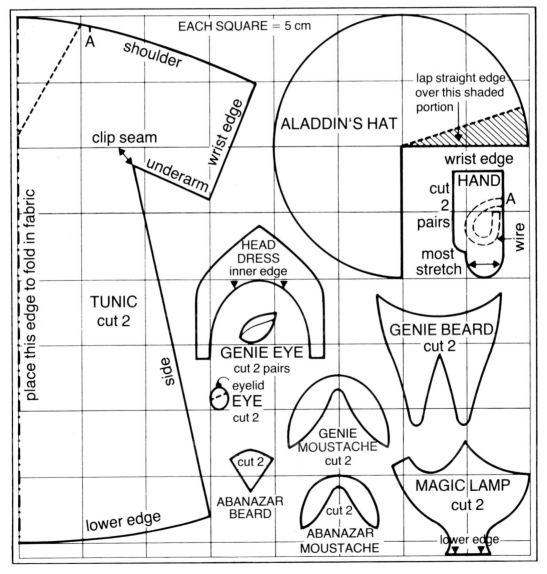

Dancing Clown

This floppy clown, about 97 cm (38 in) tall, is the perfect dancing partner for a small girl when the elastic loops on his feet are slipped over his partner's shoes. He also makes an ideal mascot doll for older children and adults

Clown

You will need: 1·10 m (1⅛ yd) of cotton stockinette – tubular knit 57 cm (22½ in) wide, opening out to 114 cm (45 in) width, (see suppliers' list on page 139). Alternatively you can use cuttings off discarded plain-knit vests and T-shirts as explained in the notes below. 500 g (1 lb) stuffing; 2 m (2 yd) of 1·5 cm (½ in) wide tape (to tie round neck and wrists and to anchor hair); a 5 by 50 cm (2 by 20 in) strip of cotton fabric (to reinforce body where arms are sewn on); 50 g ball of chunky knitting yarn for hair; two 1·5 cm (⅝ in) diameter black trouser buttons for eyes; scraps of pink felt for nose; black, blue and red thread for facial features; red pencil.

Notes: If you are making the doll from discarded vests or T-shirts, the garments available may not be large enough to cut out the pieces given in the instructions. However the pieces can be joined as necessary to make up the sizes required. For example a 38 by 56 cm (15 by 22 in) piece is needed for the body and head; this could be made up by cutting two 38 by 28·5 cm (15 by 11¼ in) pieces then joining them along one 38 cm (15 in) edge taking a 5 mm (¼ in) seam. Do take care to cut out the pieces so that the most stretch in the fabric lies in the direction stated in the instructions.

For safety, when making the doll for a very young child, use felt circles instead of buttons for the eyes and pompons in place of bells. Take 5 mm (¼ in) seams on all the doll pieces.

Body and head: Cut a 38 by 56 cm (15 by 22 in) piece of stockinette with most stretch in the fabric going across the 38 cm (15 in) width. With pencil, mark a line for neck 20 cm (8 in) down from and parallel to one 38 cm (15 in) edge, on right side of fabric – this edge will be the top of the head. Join long edges and turn right side out. Gather the top 38 cm (15 in) edge tightly and fasten off thread.

Stuff head very firmly down to neck line, then stuff remainder of body slightly more loosely, making a sausage shape 46 cm (18 in) in circumference. Turn in remaining raw edge 5 mm (¼ in), bring edges together and oversew for lower end of body. Note that the 56 cm (22 in) seam should be positioned to come at centre back of doll. Tie a length of tape as tightly as possible round marked neck line – the head should flop slightly above neck.

Face: Mark on centre position of each eye 9·5 cm (3¾ in) up from neck and set 5 cm (2 in) apart. Work a blue cross stitch, 2·5 cm (1 in) square for each eye with the mark at the centre of the cross. Work two black eyelashes in one quarter of each cross as shown in illustration.

Using a darning needle and very strong thread sew on buttons for eyes, taking thread through head from back close to one side, then through each button (with right side of button against face), then back through head; knot securely, pulling thread tight to depress buttons slightly into face.

From pink felt cut a 5 mm by 1·5 cm (¼ by ½ in) oval for nose and sew in place. With red thread work a U-shaped mouth in back stitch, 5 cm (2 in) up from neck, then oversew, working back through each stitch. Colour cheeks with pencil.

Hair: For fringe cut a 13 cm (5 in) length of tape. Wind yarn four times round two fingers of one hand, slip loops off fingers then machine stitch one end of loops to the tape. Repeat this, machining loops to tape as they are made until tape is covered. Sew tape to forehead with loops ending about 1·5 cm (½ in) above eyes.

For remainder of hair cut a 33 cm (13 in)

length of tape; make as for fringe, winding yarn round four fingers instead of two to make longer loops. Sew tape round head at back to meet fringe at front of head. Note that remainder of head will be hidden by hat later on.

Legs: For each leg cut a 20 by 46 cm (8 by 18 in) strip of stockinette with most stretch in the fabric going across the 20 cm (8 in) width. Join the long edges of each strip then turn right side out. Gather each leg tightly at one end for ankle then fasten off thread.

Stuff legs lightly so that they are flexible. Turn in top edges 5 mm ($\frac{1}{4}$ in), bring them together and oversew, then sew tops of legs securely to lower edge of body.

Arms: For each arm cut an 18 by 41 cm (7 by 16 in) strip of stockinette, with most stretch in fabric going across the 18 cm (7 in) width. Join long edges of each strip then continue stitching round one short end rounding off corners to make hand. Trim fabric at corners then turn arms right side out.

Stuff arms and finish off remaining raw edges as for legs. To make wrists, tie lengths of tape tightly round arms 10 cm (4 in) from ends of hand. Make thumbs by taking a stitch round through each hand.

To reinforce body before sewing on arms, sew the strip of cotton fabric round body about 2·5 cm (1 in) down from neck. Now sew tops of arms to each side of body 4 cm (1$\frac{1}{2}$ in) down from neck.

The clothes

You will need: 1·90 m (2 yd) of 91 cm (36 in) wide striped fabric (it doesn't matter whether stripes run across width or down length of fabric – see diagrams 1 and 2); 1·40 m (1$\frac{1}{2}$ yd) of 91 cm (36 in) wide contrast fabric for frills and rosette trimmings; 23 cm ($\frac{1}{4}$ yd) of 91 cm (36 in) wide fabric for shoes, hat band and rosette trimmings; small pieces of card and felt for shoe soles; stuffing for shoes; 1·40 m (1$\frac{1}{2}$ yd) of ric-rac braid; 30 cm (12 in) of 1·5 cm ($\frac{5}{8}$ in) wide elastic; 5 bells; adhesive; metric graph paper.

Notes: The shoe patterns are printed full size and can be traced directly off the page. To make the full size tunic pattern, copy the pattern shown in the diagram, onto graph paper noting that one square on the diagram equals 5 cm on the graph paper.

Take 1·5 cm ($\frac{5}{8}$ in) seams on the tunic pieces; other seams as stated in the instructions. Join all pieces with right side of fabric facing unless otherwise stated.

Shoes: Cut two pairs of shoe uppers. Join them in pairs taking 5 mm ($\frac{1}{4}$ in) seams at back and front. Clip seams at curves then turn shoes right side out. Cut two soles from card and two from felt. Place a card sole inside each shoe matching points A and B. Glue lower edges of shoes 5 mm ($\frac{1}{4}$ in) onto the card soles.

Stuff shoes firmly and glue the felt soles to the card soles to cover raw edges of shoe fabric. Turn in upper edges of shoes 1·5 cm ($\frac{1}{2}$ in) and place each shoe at ankle edge of each leg. Tuck gathered leg ends inside upper edge of each shoe and oversew top edges of shoes to legs.

Cut two 15 cm (6 in) lengths of elastic; sew ends of each elastic to sides of shoes (as shown on shoe upper pattern) to make loops. Now glue ric-rac braid round shoes to cover ends of elastic.

Tunic: Cut out two pairs of tunic pieces using the pattern (placing pattern on fabric as shown in diagram 1 or 2 according to direction of stripes). Join each pair of tunic pieces at centre front or back seams, then join the pairs to each other at overarm, underarm and sides. Finally bring centre seams together and join inside leg seams. Turn tunic right side out.

Wrist frills: Cut two 13 by 40 cm (5 by 16 in) strips of contrast fabric. Join short ends of each strip, then fold strips in half with right sides outside bringing long raw edges together. Sew a frill strip to each wrist edge of tunic with right sides facing, raw edges level, and taking a 5 mm ($\frac{1}{4}$ in) seam. Press seam towards tunic.

Ankle frills: Cut two 13 by 50 cm (5 by 20 in) strips of contrast fabric. Make and sew to ankle edges of tunic as instructed for wrist frills.

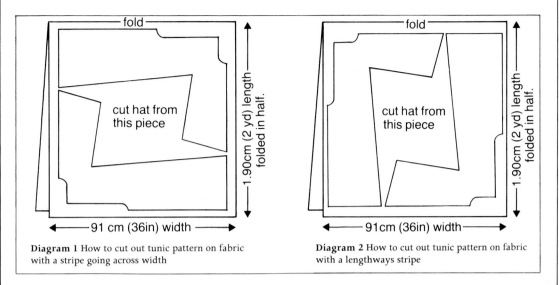

Diagram 1 How to cut out tunic pattern on fabric with a stripe going across width

Diagram 2 How to cut out tunic pattern on fabric with a lengthways stripe

To assemble doll and tunic: Place tunic on doll, turn in neck edge 1·5 cm ($\frac{5}{8}$ in) and, using strong thread, gather round close to folded edge. Pull up gathers tightly to fit neck then fasten off. Gather wrist and ankle edges in same way, running the gathering threads round through frill fabric close to seams. Catch frills through gathers to wrists and ankles all round.

Neck frills: For widest neck frill use a 23 by 136 cm (9 by 54 in) strip of fabric, joining pieces as necessary to make required length. Join all short edges then fold strip as for other frills. Turn in remaining raw edges 5 mm ($\frac{1}{4}$ in) and run a strong gathering thread round close to this edge through all thicknesses. Put frill on doll then pull up gathers to fit neck and fasten off.

For next neck frill use an 18 by 91 cm (7 by 36 in) strip, and for smallest frill use a 13 by 91 cm (5 by 36 in) strip. Make frills and sew to doll as before.

Hat: Cut two 23 by 28 cm (9 by 11 in) pieces of striped fabric and two 5 by 28 cm (2 by 11 in) strips of fabric to match shoes. Sew the narrow strips to hat pieces along the 28 cm (11 in) edges taking 5 mm ($\frac{1}{4}$ in) seam (to form band at lower edge of hat). Sew ric-rac to centre of each narrow strip of fabric. Now join side edges of hat pieces, then tightly gather up top edge and fasten off thread. Turn hat right side out.

Put hat on doll's head to cover upper looped ends of hair, turning in lower edge of hat 5 mm ($\frac{1}{4}$ in). Slip stitch lower edge of hat to head all round. Let the hat flop to one side then sew in position with a few stitches to hold in place.

Rosettes: Cut a 15 cm (6 in) diameter circle of contrast fabric for a rosette. Turn in raw edge 5 mm ($\frac{1}{4}$ in) and gather all round, pull up gathers tightly and fasten off. Sew this to gathered top of hat with a bell.

Make four more rosettes in same way – two from 18 cm (7 in) diameter circles of contrast fabric and two 10 cm (4 in) diameter circles of fabric to match shoes. Sew these in pairs to front of tunic, then sew a bell over each rosette.

For shoes, make two rosettes as for hat rosettes. Sew one to point of each shoe with a bell.

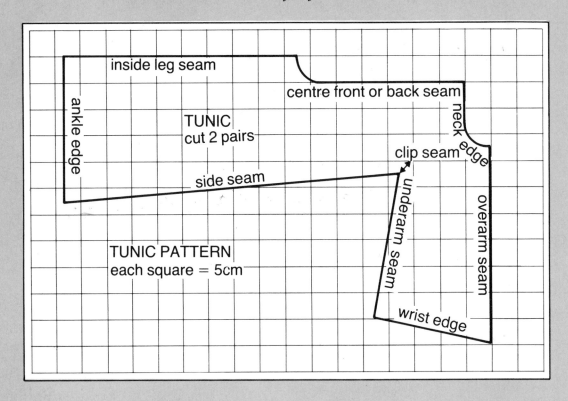

inside leg seam

centre front or back seam

ankle edge

TUNIC
cut 2 pairs

clip seam

neck edge

side seam

underarm seam

overarm seam

TUNIC PATTERN
each square = 5cm

wrist edge

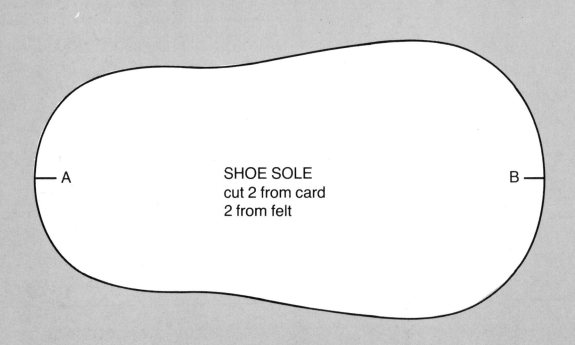

A

SHOE SOLE
cut 2 from card
2 from felt

B

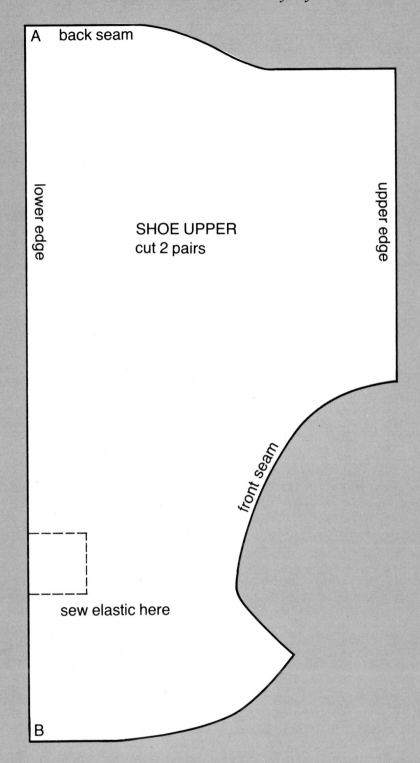

A   back seam

lower edge

upper edge

SHOE UPPER
cut 2 pairs

front seam

sew elastic here

B

Bedtime Favourites

No more tears at bedtime! Granny the hot water bottle cover and Happy Clown the pyjama case will make bedtime funtime. Granny is about 46 cm (18 in) high and the clown is 53 cm (21 in) high; they are both easy to make from scraps of dress fabrics

Granny

You will need: 25 cm ($\frac{3}{8}$ yd) of 122 cm (48 in) wide white fleecy fabric; 35 cm ($\frac{1}{2}$ yd) of printed fabric and 1·40 m ($1\frac{1}{2}$ yd) of lace edging for the dress; small pieces of pink fabric for the face and hands; scraps of black and pink felt and plain fabric; red, black, white and brown thread for embroidery; a small piece of ribbon for the bow; 3 snap fasteners; metric graph paper.

Notes: Take 1 cm ($\frac{3}{8}$ in) seams and turnings except where stated otherwise. Join fabrics with right sides facing. Copy the pattern shapes separately on to metric graph paper. Each square on diagram equals 5 cm. Cut out the shapes and use as pattern pieces.

To make: Cut the face piece from pink fabric (following the broken lines on body pattern) and mark on all facial features as shown on the pattern. Clip the upper edge then turn it in and tack.

Embroider the facial features as follows: for cheeks, use red thread and small straight stitches worked in spirals radiating from the centres. Work spectacles in chain stitch using brown thread. Work the mouth in back stitch using red thread then work back, oversewing through each stitch. Cut eyes from black felt, sew in place then embroider a small white cross on each for the highlight as shown in illustration. Cut the nose from pink felt and sew it in place.

Cut two body pieces from fleecy fabric then sew the face piece to one of them with its top edge in the position shown on the body pattern and stitching round close to the edge. Now, using black thread, machine stitch lines on hair and bun as shown in illustration, on front and back body pieces. Hem lower edge of each body piece taking a 1 cm then a 2 cm ($\frac{3}{8}$ in then $\frac{3}{4}$ in) turning.

For the dress, cut two 26 by 34 cm ($10\frac{1}{4}$ by $13\frac{1}{2}$ in) pieces of fabric. Turn in one long edge of each piece and gather until it measures 25 cm ($9\frac{3}{4}$ in). Hem the remaining long edges. Stitch the gathered edge of each dress piece to the body at position shown on body pattern. Tack side edges of dress to side edges of each body piece.

Cut four shoe pieces from plain fabric and cut two black felt pieces to shape (see dotted lines on shoe pattern). Sew these felt pieces to two of the shoe pieces. Join shoe pieces in pairs leaving upper edges open, trim seams, turn right side out then turn in upper edges and tack. Slip these upper edges 1 cm ($\frac{3}{8}$ in) under hem edge of dress at front, spacing them about 3 cm ($1\frac{1}{4}$ in) apart. Stitch upper edges of shoes in place. Sew lace trim to hem of each dress piece.

For each sleeve, cut a 12 by 20 cm ($4\frac{3}{4}$ by 8 in) strip of fabric. Join short edges of each piece and turn right side out. Cut two pairs of hand pieces from pink fabric. Join in pairs leaving upper edges open, trim seams and turn right side out. Turn in one raw edge of each sleeve and gather to fit 1 cm ($\frac{3}{8}$ in) over top of hand. Slip raw edges of hands in position inside sleeves and stitch through all

Each square = 5cm

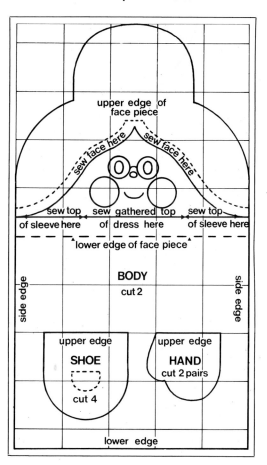

thicknesses at gathered edge. Sew lace trimming to gathers. Turn in remaining raw edges of sleeves and gather through all thicknesses to fit in positions shown on body pattern. Stitch top edges of sleeves in place then sew lace trim to neck edge of each dress piece.

Join body pieces all round, leaving lower edges open and catching side edges of dress in seams but taking care not to catch sleeves in seams. Sew snap fasteners to lower edges of body pieces and a small ribbon bow to front of bun.

The Clown

You will need: Small pieces of white stockinette for head and hands (cuttings from an old T-shirt can be used); 50 cm of 91 cm ($\frac{5}{8}$ yd of 36 in) wide fabric for body and sleeves; 40 cm of 91 cm ($\frac{1}{2}$ yd of 36 in) wide fabric for frills; small pieces of felt for hat and shoes; scraps of black, pink and red felt plus black, white and red thread for facial features; a bell or bobble for top of cap; three bobbles for front of body; 250 g ($\frac{1}{2}$ lb) of stuffing; 35 cm ($\frac{1}{2}$ yd) of trimming for hat; three large snap fasteners; chunky yarn for hair; adhesive; metric graph paper.

Notes: Make patterns as for Granny. Cut out head and hands with most stretch in stockinette in direction shown on patterns. Take 1 cm ($\frac{3}{8}$ in) seams and turnings throughout. Join fabrics with right sides facing.

To make the head: Cut two head pieces from stockinette. Join the side edges then run a gathering thread round 1 cm ($\frac{3}{8}$ in) from the top edge. Pull up gathers tightly and fasten off securely. Turn head right side out and stuff to measure about 36 cm (14 in) round. Bring neck edges together and run a gathering thread through both thicknesses along the dotted line shown on pattern. Pull up gathers until neck measures 5 cm (2 in) across then fasten off.

Cut nose from red felt, eyes from black felt and cheeks from pink felt. Work a highlight on each eye using white thread as shown in the illustration. Use dabs of adhesive to hold

the features in position as follows: place nose 7 cm ($2\frac{3}{4}$ in) up from the neck edge; eyes at either side of the nose and 4 cm ($1\frac{1}{2}$ in) apart; cheeks below eyes as illustrated. Work a shallow W shape 2 cm ($\frac{3}{4}$ in) below nose using red thread. Sew all features in place then work four straight black stitches out from each eye to form a cross as illustrated.

For hair, wind yarn five times round three fingers then slip loops off fingers. Back stitch tops of loops to right side of head, covering the seam and level with top of eye. Continue making loops in this way round back of head to other side. Repeat this process making another row of loops 2 cm ($\frac{3}{4}$ in) above the first row. When you reach the other side of the head, continue making loops across the forehead, winding the yarn round two fingers instead of three for the fringe.

Cut four hat pieces from felt and join them in pairs at one side edge then join the pairs at the remaining side edges. Trim seams and turn right side out. Stuff top of hat and place on head lapping tops of yarn loops with lower edge of hat. Sew hat to head all round adding more stuffing to shape it if necessary. Sew bell to top of hat and trimming to lower edge.

The hands: Cut two pairs of hand pieces and join them leaving wrist edges open. Trim seams and turn right side out. Stuff hands then run gathering threads round wrist edges. Pull up gathers and fasten off.

The shoes: Make as for hands, gathering upper edges.

The body: Cut out body pieces and sleeves as stated on patterns. Join body back pieces from A to B and C to D. Press seam to one side then turn in and stitch back raw edges to neaten. Join sleeves in pairs at upper and underarm edges. Turn right side out and tack armhole edges of each sleeve together pulling stitches to gather to fit between points indicated on body pattern. Tack armhole edges of sleeves to side edges of front body piece having raw edges level. Now join body back to front at side edges catching armhole edges of sleeves in seams. Join front to back at inside leg edges then clip seam at point D. Turn body right side out and sew snap fasteners to back edges.

Turn in neck edge of body and gather. Pull up gathers to fit round gathered neck edge of head then fasten off. Sew gathered neck edge of body securely to neck all round. Turn in and gather wrist and ankle edges of body in the same way pulling up gathers to fit over hands and shoes lapping them about 2 cm ($\frac{3}{4}$ in). Push a little stuffing inside each sleeve then sew gathered edges of the clown's body to the hands and shoes all round.

Sew bobbles to front of body.

The frills: For neck frill cut a 16 by 91 cm ($6\frac{1}{4}$ by 36 in) strip of fabric. Join long edges of strip then turn right side out. Turn in short edges at ends of strip then slip stitch ends together. Run a gathering thread round the seamed edge of frill and place frill round neck. Pull up gathers to fit neck tightly then fasten off.

For each wrist frill cut an 8 by 35 cm (3 by $13\frac{3}{4}$ in) strip of fabric and for each ankle frill cut a 10 by 45 cm (4 by $17\frac{3}{4}$ in) strip of fabric. Make as for the neck frill and after placing in position sew gathered edges of these frills to the wrists and ankles of the doll.

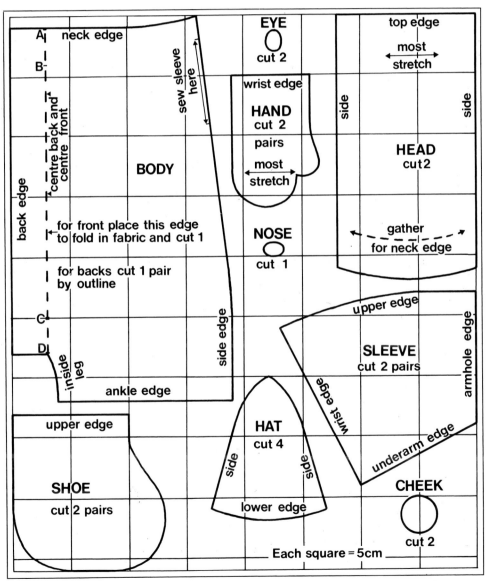

Funny Bunny

This cuddly bunny doubles as a teaching toy. He is dressed in clothes that have buttons and braces, buckle and laces, poppers and a zip fastner. He is 63 cm (25 in) high and his T-shirt is decorated with a clockface with movable hands – a fun way for any child to learn to tell the time

The rabbit

You will need: 50 cm (about $\frac{1}{2}$ yd) of Acrilan or Courtelle fleece fabric, 122 cm (48 in) wide; 500 g (1 lb) stuffing; scraps of stiff fabric such as Vilene interlining, to interline ears; scraps of red, black and pink felt, and black yarn for facial features; small pieces of fabric, felt, stiff card and a thick boot lace 91 cm (36 in) long for shoes; adhesive; metric graph paper.

Notes: 5 mm ($\frac{1}{4}$ in) seams are allowed on all pieces unless otherwise stated. Join pieces with right sides of fabric facing unless otherwise stated.

When binding raw edges with bias binding, turn bias completely to inside so that it cannot be seen on the right side of the garment.

On to metric graph paper copy the patterns square by square (each square on diagram equals 2 cm).

To make: From the patterns cut out body and ear pieces as directed, in fleece. For arms cut four fleece pieces 23·5 cm (9$\frac{1}{4}$ in) long by 7·5 cm (3 in) wide. Round off corners at one short end of each piece for hand.

Join body pieces round edges, stitching along line indicated between legs, leaving a gap in seam at one side, and leaving lower leg edges open as shown on pattern. Clip fabric between legs and clip seam at neck. Turn right side out. Stuff body and head firmly, then ladder-stitch opening in seam.

Cut shoe pieces in fabric. Join them in pairs at front and back seams; leaving upper and lower edges open. Trim seams and turn right side out. Cut two soles from card and place one inside each shoe at lower edge, matching points A and B. Glue lower edges of shoes 5 mm ($\frac{1}{4}$ in) on to card soles. Glue a felt sole to

each shoe to cover raw edges of fabric. Stuff shoes firmly.

Turn in upper edges of each shoe 5 mm ($\frac{1}{4}$ in), place these edges slightly overlapping lower edges of legs, with shoes turned outwards slightly, so that the rabbit will stand with toes apart, heels together. Slip stitch shoes to legs, adding more stuffing as you go to make legs and shoes quite firm.

Cut bootlace in half to make two equal lengths. Neaten cut ends by rolling strips of sticky tape tightly round. Sew centre of each shoe lace to each shoe in a triangular shape (as shown in illustration), so that ends are free to be knotted and tied.

Tie strong thread as tightly as possible round rabbit's neck to shape it, then sew thread ends into body.

Using black yarn, mark mouth in long straight stitches: begin about 9 cm (3$\frac{1}{2}$ in) up from neck and work a fairly long stitch downwards, then make shorter stitches for lower part of mouth as shown in the illustrations.

For a nose cut a 3 cm (1$\frac{1}{4}$ in) long oval of red felt and sew this in place covering top of first mouth stitch. For eyes cut two 2·5 cm (1 in) diameter circles of black felt; pin them in place each side of nose, about 4·5 cm (1$\frac{3}{4}$ in) apart, then work black eyelashes before sewing the eyes in place. Cut two pink felt circles 5 cm (2 in) diameter, and sew them in place to make cheeks.

Join ear pieces in threes, placing one interlining piece against each pair of fleece pieces (right sides facing) and leaving lower edges open. Trim seams and turn right side out. Turn in lower edges and slip stitch, pulling thread tight to gather slightly. Ladder stitch ears firmly in places shown on pattern.

Join arm pieces in pairs, leaving short straight edges open. Turn right side out and

134

stuff to within 5 cm (2 in) of top. Tie strong thread round wrists 6·5 cm (2½ in) up from hands as for neck. Turn in upper edges of arms, bringing seams together, and slip stitch pulling thread to gather slightly. Sew arms to body at each side, 4 cm (1½ in) below neck.

The rabbit's clothes

T-shirt

You will need: 30 cm (about ⅜ yd) of fabric 91 cm (36 in) wide; bias binding for neatening raw edges; a strip of Velcro touch and close fastener, 18 cm (7 in) long; scraps of white Vilene interlining, felt and a button for clock motif; adhesive.

To make: Cut two T-shirt pieces from fabric as shown on pattern, then cut one open on fold line for back opening of shirt.

For the clock face cut a circle of Vilene 7 cm (2¾ in) diameter; mark numerals round it with a ball-point pen. Stick, then sew clock face to a 7·5 cm (3 in) diameter circle of felt, then stick and sew a 5 cm (2 in) diameter circle of felt to centre of clock. For clock hands stick a small piece of felt on to Vilene, then cut out two 5 mm (¼ in) wide strips, one 3 cm (1¼ in) long and the other 2·5 cm (1 in) long. Cut ends of hands to a point, and make a small hole at opposite end of each hand, with scissor points. Sew hands to clock face, taking thread through these holes, through the button and back again through the holes. The hands can now be moved to any position. Stitch clock to centre front of T-shirt 4 cm (1½ in) down from neck edge.

Join T-shirt front to backs at shoulder seams, then sew one edge of bias to sleeve edges. Join underarm and side seams, stitching twice to reinforce, then clip seams as shown on pattern. Finish off binding sleeve edges then bind lower and neck edges. Turn in back edges 5 mm (¼ in), and sew on Velcro strips to fasten.

Pants

You will need: 20 cm (about ¼ yd) of fabric 91 cm (36 in) wide; scraps of leathercloth or felt for braces; two large buttons.

To make: Cut two pairs of pants pieces from fabric. Join them in pairs at centre seams, clipping curves in seams. Join these pairs to each other at side seams, then inside leg seams. Turn in waist and lower edges 5 mm (¼ in) twice, and hem.

For braces cut two strips 41 cm (16 in) long by 4 cm (1½ in) wide. (If felt is used stitch together two layers for strength.) Round off one end of each strip and cut a large oval slit in these ends, starting 2·5 cm (1 in) in from the ends, to fit buttons easily.

Sew buttons to pants at front, where shown on pattern. Put pants on rabbit and loop buttonhole ends of braces on to buttons. Take braces back over each shoulder, cross them over at centre back and tuck ends inside back waist edge of pants, pinning and adjusting length to fit neatly. Take off pants and sew back edges of braces in place, trimming off any excess length.

The jacket

You will need: 70 cm (about ¾ yd) of fabric 91 cm (36 in) wide; an open-ended zip fastener long enough to be cut to fit jacket; bias binding for neatening raw edges; a buckle; metal eyelets (optional).

To make: Cut two jacket pieces from fabric as directed on pattern, then cut one piece in half along fold line for centre front opening. Cut two pockets from fabric. Turn in upper edges of pockets 1·5 cm (½ in) and stitch. Turn in remaining raw edges 5 mm (¼ in) and tack. Sew pockets to front of jacket as shown on pattern.

Open the zip fastener. Turn in centre front edges of jacket fronts 5 mm (¼ in) and tack them each side of zip fastener, with lower edges of zip 1·5 cm (½ in) above lower raw edges of jacket fronts. Cut top ends of zip level with neck edges. After this *do not* close the zip right up until the collar is sewn on or the slide fastener will come off.

With the zip fastener undone, machine one half of it to each front edge of the jacket, then remove the tacking stitches.

Join jacket fronts to back at shoulder seams. Sew one edge of bias to lower sleeve edges. Join side and underarm seams, sewing twice to reinforce, then clip seams at underarms.

Finish off binding on lower sleeve edges then bind lower edge of jacket.

Cut two collar pieces and join them leaving neck edges open. Trim seam, turn right side out and press. Tack raw edges of collar to neck edge of jacket, lining up the ends of the collar with the centre front edges of the jacket. Stitch bias binding over the join on inside of jacket, taking care to stitch between zip teeth.

Note: To avoid striking zip teeth with machine needle, one or two teeth can be pulled right off the fastener.

For the belt cut a strip of fabric 69 cm (27 in) long, and twice as wide as centre bar of buckle, plus 1·5 cm ($\frac{1}{2}$ in). Join long edges of strip and sew across one end, making a V point. Turn right side out and press. Attach buckle to other end of belt, making a small hole for prong. Pin belt to jacket 5·5 cm ($2\frac{1}{4}$ in) above lower edge, with buckle at centre front. Sew belt to jacket to within 2·5 cm (1 in) of centre front edges. Put eyelets in end of belt, or cut small holes and buttonhole stitch to neaten.

Carrots

You will need some scraps of orange and green fabric and stuffing; a large snap fastener.

As a pattern use one quarter of a circle 20 cm (8 in) in diameter. Cut two carrots in orange fabric. Join straight edges of each piece, turn right side out and stuff. For each carrot top, fray out one long edge of a small strip of green fabric. Roll up the strips and put one inside each carrot top, unfrayed edges downwards. Run a gathering thread round each carrot top, pull up tightly turning in raw edges, and fasten off thread securely. Put one carrot in jacket pocket. Sew half a snap fastener to remaining carrot and other half to rabbit's hand.

Scarf

Use a strip of fabric 15 cm (6 in) by 91 cm (36 in). Fray out the short edges then join long edges of strip. Turn right side out. Press, then stitch across short ends above fringes.

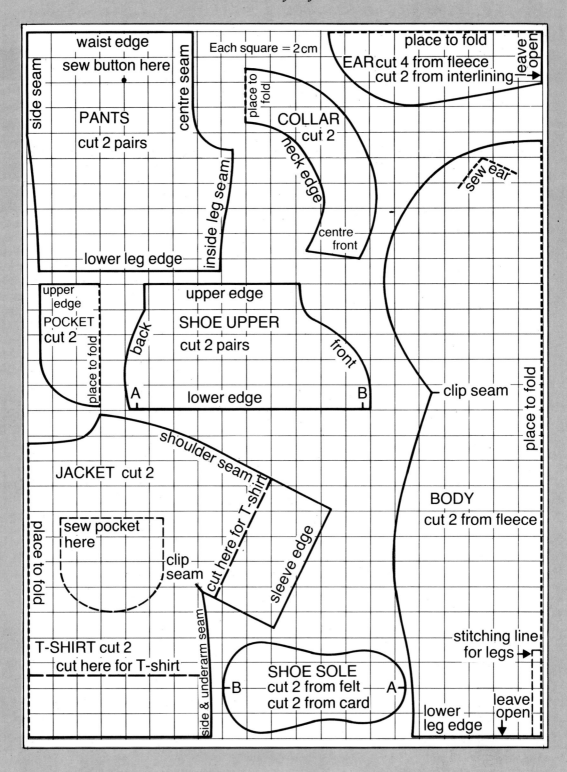

LIST OF SUPPLIERS

Beckfoot Mill,
Howden Road,
Silsden,
Nr. Keighley,
West Yorkshire BD20 0HA
Tel. no. (0535) 53358 or 52244

For fur fabric, felt, fillings, stockinette, joints
and all other toymaking accessories.
Send 50p for complete catalogue (refunded on
first order).

Griffin Fabrics Ltd.,
The Craft Centre,
97 Claremont Street,
Aberdeen AB1 6QR
Tel. no. (0224) 20798

For fur fabric, felt, fillings, stockinette, joints
and all other toymaking accessories.
Send 50p for complete catalogue (refunded on
first order).

INDEX

Page numbers in italics refer to colour illustrations

Abanazar, *118*, 122
adhesive, 11
    removing, 11
Aladdin, *118*, 120–1

Bee, *62*, 64
Bunny, *62*, 64
    Mr and Mrs, 40–4, *43*
    Teaching Toy, 134–8, *135*

compasses, 11
circles, drawing, *12*
    gathering, 16, *16*
closing openings, 17
Clown:
    Dancing, 124–9, *126*
    pyjama case, *130*, 132–3
colouring cheeks, 14
Cowboy, 108, *110*
Cowgirl, 109–111, *110*
Cows, miniature (Moo and
    Chew), 67–9, *67*

Dog, *62*, 66
    Soulful Hound, 31–3, *31*
dressmaking equipment, 11
Dutch Dolls, *98*, 100–2

equipment, 11

facial features, 14, 17
felt, 13
    cutting out, *13*
fillings for toys, 16
fur fabric, 13
    pinning, *13*

Genies, *118*, 122–3
Granny, hot water bottle cover,
    130–2, *130*

hair for dolls, 14
Hedgehog, *62*, 65

Horse, *110*, 111
hot water bottle case, 130–2,
    130
Humpty Dumpty, 23–5, *23*

Koala, *62*, 65

ladder stitch, 17, *17*
Ladybird, 59–61, *59*, *62*, 64
limbs, attaching, 17, *17*, *20*
Lion, *62*, 66
    Leo the Laughing, *54*, 56–8
lumpy toys, 16

measurements, 11
Mouse, *62*, 65

Nightdress Case Doll, *79*, 81–2
Novelty Toys, 119–138

Octopus, *62*, 64
Owl, *62*, 65

Panda, Mother and Baby, 45–7,
    46
patterns, copying, 12
    drawing out, *12*
Penguin, *62*, 66
Princess, *118*, 121–2
Puppets for a Pantomime, *118*,
    119–23
Pushchair, 48, 50, *51*
Puss in Boots, 26–30, *26*
pyjama case, *130*, 132–3

Rabbit, *62*, 64 (*see also* Bunny)
    Teaching Toy, 134–8, *135*
Rag Dolls, 70–97
    Adaptable, 79–83, *79*
    Dressing-up *79*, 80–1
    fabrics for, 14
    Glad-rag, 90–7, *90*
    making, 14

Nightdress Case, *79*, 81–2
    Topsy-turvy, *79*, 82
    Twins, *70*, 72–8
    Well-dressed, 84–9, *86*, *87*
Rosette dolls, *15*, 99–117
    Dutch, *98*, 100–2
    Home on the Range, 108–13,
        110
    making, 15–16
    materials, 15
    Sam and Sue Scarecrow,
        103–7, *103*
    Turnabout Doll, 114–7, *114*
rosette, finished, 16
ruler, 11

safety first, 11
Scarecrows, 103–7, *103*
seams, 13, *13*
smooth stroke of fur pile, 13
stockinette, 14
stuffing the toy, 16

Teaching Toy, 134–8, *135*
Teddy Bears:
    Koala, *62*, 65
    Mascot, 34–9, *34*, *35*
    Mother and Baby, 48–53, *49*,
        51
    Superbear, *35*, 36–9
    Traditional, jointed, *18*, 20–2
    Twinkletoes, *34*, 36–9
templates, 16
Topsy-turvy Doll, *79*, 82
Tortoise, *62*, 64
Turnabout Dolly, 114–7, *114*
tweezers, 11

Widow Twankey, *118*, 122

yarns, 14